What People Are Saying About Paul Solarz and

LEARN
LIKE A
PIRATE

"Would your class fall apart without you? Could your students learn if you didn't speak for an entire day? In *Learn Like a PIRATE*, Paul Solarz shares methods you can use to create a student-led classroom and prepare your students for a lifetime of self-led learning."

—**DANIEL H. PINK**, author of *Drive* and *A Whole New Mind*

"While many teachers tend to be at the helm of the ship, *Learn Like a PIRATE* is a model for teaching from the crow's nest: having a clear vantage point of the class and its direction, but letting students steer their learning. Paul has recaptured the 'pirate' spirit in his own way. Diving into the activities of his classroom, we see how students take charge of their learning—and how daring teachers make it happen."

—**ANGELA MAIERS**, Founder of Choose2Matter and author of *The Passion-Driven Classroom*

"For learning to be relevant and meaningful in the eyes of students today, school experiences need to be more learner centric. Paul Solarz has crafted the perfect guide to help invigorate classroom learning experiences to empower students to take ownership over their learning."

—**ERIC SHENINGER**, Senior Fellow at the International Center for Leadership in Education and author of *Digital Leadership*

"In *Learn Like a PIRATE*, Paul Solarz explains how to design classroom experiences that encourage students to take risks and explore their passions in a stimulating, motivating, and supportive environment where improvement, rather than grades, is the focus. The particular techniques (and the underlying philosophy) he offers are highly consistent with teaching practice at the distinguished level in my Framework for Teaching. In that model, I tried to describe, at the distinguished level, classrooms in which the teacher has created a community of learners, with the students themselves assuming much of the responsibility for what occurs there. Mr. Solarz offers specific ideas for how to accomplish that."

—**CHARLOTTE DANIELSON**, author of *Enhancing Professional Practice*

"As I read *Learn Like A PIRATE*, I regretted that I was not teaching in the classroom where I would be able to work with students in the thoughtful and imaginative ways he suggests. It is rare that we have a firsthand report of the day-to-day practicalities of transforming classes into places where students can become self-directed, curious, interdependent learners. Paul has succeeded in sharing his passion for authentic twenty-first century teaching as well as inspiring us to imitate and invent our own models for preparing our students for an increasingly complex world of invention and problem solving."

—**BENA KALLICK**, co-Director of the Institute for Habits of Mind and co-author of the *Habits of Mind* books

"There are countless books and articles on how to change school systems to pave the way for twenty-first century education, and most of them are, at best, wishful thinking for an implicitly distant future. Paul Solarz's book is invaluable in that it tells the real life story of how he is doing that right now in his classroom."

—**GABRIEL RSHAID**, Professional Development Associate at The Leadership and Learning Center and author of *The 21st-Century Classroom*

"Paul Solarz does amazing inquiry work with elementary students. If you ever thought, 'Oh my students are too young for that,' then check out Paul's site and his writing on inquiry and project-based learning in the classroom. Paul is a go to resource on Passion Time, Genius Hour, and Inquiry-Based learning at the elementary level."

—A.J. JULIANI, author of *Learning by Choice*

"Paul is a top-notch superstar in the education world. Paul could easily be at the top of anyone's list for educator of the year. He believes strongly in the incorporation of twenty-first century skills, giving students autonomy, challenging students to make a positive impact on the world, and then he showcases their work to the world. Every time I visit Paul's website, my head hurts because he has so many wonderful ideas and projects that he does with his students. I believe his students are very lucky to have someone that is truly preparing them to be successful in the real world and setting a great example as a hard-working, passionate, compassionate, game changer."

—OLIVER SCHINKTEN, co-Founder of Communities program and ComPassion Based Learning model, and Founder of AssistEd Shift

"As an educator, I often get most of my professional development from many other experienced and risk-taking educators within my own community and around the country. Through social media, I came across a truly innovative educator, Paul Solarz, who utilizes these twenty-first century skills into his daily lessons. His willingness to share has helped me and many other educators advance our own practice."

—STEPHANIE DWYER, seventh grade English Teacher

"Anybody who knows teachers on Twitter will know of Paul—he is someone I aspire to be when I 'grow up' as a teacher. For the amazing work he does with 'Genius Hour,' his class library that I don't so secretly covet, and so many more reasons, he is one of the first I go to when I have a question, because most times he will either know the answer or he will point me in the right direction.

—**CATHY DOHN**, Elementary Teacher

"In Paul's classroom, students are actively engaged in what they learn. The environment is collaborative, upbeat, and productive. Students are empowered to take risks and learn from their mistakes, as well as their successes. Paul is highly respected by his students, their parents, and fellow educators worldwide."

—**PAULA SULLIVAN**, 5th grade co-worker

LEARN
LIKE A
PIRATE

EMPOWER YOUR STUDENTS
TO COLLABORATE, LEAD, AND SUCCEED

By Paul Solarz

Learn Like a Pirate

© 2015 by Paul Solarz

This book is available at special discounts when purchased in quantity for use as premiums, promotions, fundraising, and educational use. For inquiries and details, contact us: daveburgessconsulting@gmail.com.

Published by Dave Burgess Consulting, Inc.
San Diego, CA
http://daveburgessconsulting.com

Cover Design by Genesis Kohler
Interior Design by My Writers' Connection

Library of Congress Control Number: 2015933027
ISBN TPB: 978-0-9882176-6-9
ISBN eBook: 978-0-9882176-7-6

First Printing: March 2015

DEDICATION

This book is dedicated to my niece, Ashley, and my nephew, Tyler, whom I love as if they were my own children. It's also dedicated to my sister, Amy, and brother-in-law, Justin, who invite me to all of their children's activities so I can be a part of their lives. Finally, this book is dedicated to my parents: my mom, whose child-centered, avant-garde parenting style I've chosen to transform into a teaching philosophy, and my dad, whose determined work ethic and selfless nature inspired me to be the best teacher I could be.

While writing Learn Like a PIRATE, my family and I suffered a tremendous loss. My father passed away while driving home from work one evening. He was sixty-two and was loved by everyone who knew him. Our family has so many wonderful memories together. We're most thankful for the vacation we took as a family to the Dominican Republic in 2014—it was the only thing left on his bucket list! He loved his life, his job, and his family, especially his grandchildren, with whom he talked or visited every single day! I am so thankful for the thirty-eight years I got to spend with him. I love you, Dad!

LAY OF THE LAND

ACKNOWLEDGMENTS

I am grateful to so many people for their help in accomplishing my dream of publishing a book! I want to thank:

My publishers, Dave and Shelley Burgess, who gave me the opportunity to write a book in the PIRATE family.

My editor, Erin Casey, for transforming my chicken scratches into intelligible thoughts fit for publishing.

My principal, Caz Badynee, for getting me onto Twitter and helping me put together the best Professional Learning Network imaginable! His continued support and encouragement play a large role in my desire and ability to constantly improve my craft.

My assistant principal, Sue Klarner, for always making small accomplishments feel huge! You can always see in her eyes how much she cares about the teachers and students at Westgate.

My district administration staff, especially Lori Bein, Eric Olson, Jake Chung, and Chris Fahnoe for their vision, kindness, and support. They are leading our district in a very positive direction and each is doing so with class and a smile.

My co-workers who put up with the noise coming from my classroom and the laptop cart always being checked out, in addition to hundreds of other things! I'm so lucky to work with people I consider to be some of my closest friends!

My students and their parents for supporting me through the years as I experimented and took chances every day in the classroom. Their positive feedback and heartfelt opinions about PIRATE learning can be found throughout this book.

My family and friends for being so supportive and understanding as I've put in hundreds of hours writing and revising *Learn Like a Pirate* during the past six months. I'm tremendously blessed to have so many loved ones in my life!

FOREWORD

I have a confession. I did not have a student-led classroom. Hopefully I created a classroom that was engaging, meaningful, fun, and a life-changing experience for my students...but student-led? No.

I also realize empowering students to lead, collaborate, own their learning, and develop twenty-first century skills is a critical component of education, so I wanted to add another voice to the pirate family. Paul Solarz was an easy choice to be that voice. Countless times, teachers have mentioned to me the positive impact Paul's resources and online collaboration have had on their classes. He has been a huge contributor to the #tlap *(Teach Like a PIRATE)* community, and I was honored he accepted the challenge to write this book.

In *Learn Like a PIRATE*, Paul swings open the door of his classroom and not only shows us exactly how he builds his student-led culture from the ground up, but also delivers a persuasive pitch as to why. One thing will become clear right away; Paul actually does this stuff! He is a practitioner. He is still in his classroom every day walking the talk. It's that realness that I believe will resonate with other teachers and administrators.

Paul has completely reworked my original PIRATE acronym to perfectly fit his powerful message of student empowerment. This is a treasure map that, if followed, will allow you to design a class that not only covers your content, but also prepares students to lead and thrive in a rapidly changing world. Education isn't just about raising test scores; it's about raising human potential. Paul has truly embraced the notion that teaching is a mighty purpose and that transforming lives is at the heart of this worthy profession.

In the #tlap community, we talk a lot of talk about how risk-taking and stepping out of our comfort zones is what PIRATE educators do. Well, it turns out that perhaps the most daring maneuver a pirate captain can make is to be willing to hand over the wheel and let the crew steer the ship.

Dave Burgess
President of Dave Burgess Consulting, Inc.
Author of *Teach Like a PIRATE*
co-Author of *P is for PIRATE*

*"Give a man a fish and you feed him for a day.
Teach a man to fish and you feed him for a lifetime."*
Chinese Proverb

*"Tell me and I forget. Teach me and I remember.
Involve me and I learn."*
Benjamin Franklin

*"Talk at me and I struggle to learn. Actively involve
me and I achieve. Empower me to lead and I take my
new skills wherever I go."*
Paul Solarz

GET MORE OUT OF
LEARN LIKE A PIRATE

In the following pages, you'll find all sorts of ideas, tips, lessons, and strategies for creating an environment that empowers students to collaborate, lead, and succeed in your classroom—and ultimately, in life. A few of the tactics I've shared are completely original, but many are methods I've learned from others and adapted to suit my teaching style, goals, and students' needs. I encourage you to take the same approach!

Why start from scratch when you can commandeer ideas and strategies and use them as your own? Think of it as the pirate's version of collaboration! To make implementation easy, I've provided QR codes throughout this book (and clickable links for those of you reading this in digital format). Each will take you to corresponding images, videos, blog posts, or other resources so you can see exactly how these concepts can be applied in your classroom.

Visit LearnLikeAPirate.com for even more resources. You can also find me on Twitter, @PaulSolarz, and join #LearnLAP chats to expand your thinking and your Professional Learning Network (PLN).

LEARN LIKE A PIRATE

INTRODUCTION

When I became a teacher more than fifteen years ago, I was told my main purpose was to prepare my fifth-grade students for middle school. Taking that task to heart, I began a quest to determine the traits a middle schooler needed. I discovered they should be academically prepared for complex assignments, mentally prepared for interdisciplinary projects, socially prepared for pre-adolescent experiences, and emotionally mature enough to handle the challenges they would face in the coming school year.

Teachers learn right along with their students, and I learned early on that it wasn't possible for me to tell my students everything they needed to know. I can't force my students to learn and mature academically, socially, and emotionally. But I can offer incredible experiences that make them eager to learn. I can provide a space that gives them the confidence to step outside their comfort zones and try new things. And I can help my students grow by creating a classroom culture in which they have ownership of their learning.

No matter what grade they teach, all teachers want to help their students to mature academically, socially, and emotionally. The process looks different at each grade level, but the desired outcome is the same. I believe the best way to help students learn and grow is to challenge them to take responsibility for their learning experiences through student-led classrooms. *Learn Like a PIRATE* explains how and why I have created a student-led learning environment in my classroom. I hope this book inspires you to try this approach in your classroom. If you do, I'm confident you'll discover how much children can learn when they're empowered to run the show!

So, why is the book called *Learn Like a PIRATE*? Dave Burgess explains in his book *Teach Like a PIRATE* (a book I highly recommend) what it means to have the spirit of a pirate:

> *"Pirates are daring, adventurous, and willing to set forth into uncharted territories with no guarantee of success. They reject the status quo and refuse to conform to any society that stifles creativity and independence. They are entrepreneurs who take risks and are willing to travel to the ends of the earth for that which they value. Although fiercely independent, they travel with and embrace a diverse crew. If you're willing to live by the code, commit to the voyage, and pull your share of the load, then you're free to set sail. Pirates don't much care about public perception; they proudly fly their flags in defiance. And besides, everybody loves a pirate."*

As teachers, we need the traits of a pirate. Likewise, our students need the characteristics of confidence, curiosity, independence, and collaboration so they can be successful not only in school, but throughout their lives. Unfortunately, the current state of education tends to stifle, rather than foster, a pirate-like attitude.

- Students need to become risk-takers, but systems and classrooms that prioritize grades above all else foster a fear of failure.

- Students need to make creative decisions, but rigid rules and step-by-step directions stifle creativity and innovation.

- Students need to learn to work well with others, but they can't develop interpersonal skills working alone or listening to the teacher all day.

Learn Like a PIRATE challenges current education models and is intended to encourage and equip teachers of all grade levels. It is my belief that with the proper motivation and the appropriate amount of freedom, your students will rise to the challenge and impress you. Teachers of third grade and above should have little trouble implementing the strategies outlined in this book. Even students in primary grades (K-2) will benefit from opportunities to run portions of their studies, take initiative, and develop leadership skills.

The methods shared in *Learn Like a PIRATE* are probably very different from those you were taught in college. The experiences shared here may look very unlike that of your current classroom. I encourage you to read this book with an open mind and consider how you could implement or adapt the ideas for your unique students and circumstances. Determine what "student-led" could look like in your classroom, and then give it a shot. You need only one student who is brave enough to try to lead the class and the rest will follow! Be patient. They are sure to make lots of mistakes early on, but the payoff is worth it. I promise! By equipping them to take ownership of their education, you are making a huge difference in your students' lives. What better way could you fulfill your true responsibility as a teacher than by empowering children to become lifelong learners and independent thinkers?

Are you ready to begin the journey? Great! Let's set sail!

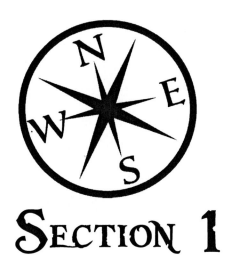

SECTION 1

THE STUDENT-LED CLASSROOM

WHAT IS A STUDENT-LED CLASSROOM?

"Right is right, even if no one is doing it;
wrong is wrong even if everyone is doing it."

—Augustine of Hippo

"Yesss!" exclaims an excited student, holding up his hand to his classmates in an offer of celebration. High-fives and words of encouragement pass around the group of four students before they turn back to their project. All around the classroom, clusters of three and four students work together, deeply engaged in meaningful work. As the boys and girls share ideas, no one fears being called "stupid." Instead, they listen to one another's opinions and ask one another questions without worry. Rather than bickering about getting their way, the students use conflict-management techniques and speak respectfully to each other. The teacher moves from group to group to hear what each is discussing. Suddenly, a student from one of those groups calls out, "Give me five! Give me five!" and everyone goes silent for the moment, waiting for the direction or announcement or question, and then quickly gets back to work.

Engaged children working together on meaningful tasks; this is what my classroom looks like after approximately two to three weeks of school. My job is to stoke this spirit of collaboration so that my students thrive all school year long.

A STUDENT-LED CLASSROOM IS ONE IN WHICH STUDENTS MAKE DECISIONS AND CHOICES THROUGHOUT THE DAY WITHOUT CONSULTING THE TEACHER.

I know I'm not alone in this goal. Many teachers today diligently work to eliminate the stereotype of students sitting in rows, completing worksheet after worksheet, only getting a break from the silent monotony to listen to a lecture they find uninteresting and irrelevant. Looking for a new way to teach, these forward-thinking educators seek to involve students in the learning process. They want to encourage students to take on more responsibility and ownership over their learning. Because you've picked up this book, I suspect you are one of these world-changing teachers. And you may be wondering where and how to begin.

Going against the flow isn't easy. Resistance is a natural response to new ideas and methods. That's particularly true in the educational system. Throughout my teaching career, I have relied on a non-traditional, student-led classroom to meet my students' needs. This approach has worked effectively for more than fifteen years, even though the mix of students and their abilities and personalities has changed dramatically from year to year. Despite consistent success, other teachers warn me year after year that my style of teaching won't work during the next year. Some claim that the particular mix of children isn't well suited for student-led environments. Other teachers have told me that particular students cannot survive in my classroom. Year after year, I've proven that with a consistent message and belief, a student-led classroom environment is attainable—and it's what children deserve. A student-led classroom is one in which students make decisions and choices throughout the day without consulting the teacher.

These decisions impact their own actions, the actions of others, and even the actions of the teacher. Everyone in the classroom appears to have equal power and equal say in what happens, although everyone understands that the teacher's word is final.

So what? Do the kids just come into class every day and decide what to learn and how they want to learn it? No. Depending on the subject, most lessons include a component of teacher-led instruction (often a mini-lesson in the middle of the period), as well as collaborative work time (with regular feedback from their peers and the teacher) and time to reflect or synthesize. The curricular objectives don't change—the method does. Lessons are set up so that students don't have to be passive learners for long. The teacher says what needs to be said and then gets out of the way, allowing students ample opportunity to guide and lead one another.

PRACTICE MAKES PERMANENT, SO HELP THEM PRACTICE CORRECTLY!

Creating a student-led classroom doesn't happen overnight. It requires a tremendous amount of commitment from both the teacher and the students. To get to the point where each student feels comfortable directing the class without consulting the teacher, lots of instruction and practice must take place. Teachers need to explain what a student-led classroom is and provide examples of how it might work for them. Every day, teachers need to provide learning opportunities for students to practice the necessary skills until they become habits. In addition, teachers must give encouraging feedback when students make positive decisions and supportive feedback when negative decisions are made. It is also extremely important to show appreciation for any attempt made despite the outcome in order to ensure that they try again in the near future! Practice makes permanent, so help them practice correctly!

One final note: Student-led classrooms are only effective if students feel safe, appreciated, and connected to their teacher. In my classroom, we talk about being a family on a regular basis. I show my students I care for them through informal conversations before and after school, taking a genuine interest in their passions, and providing time for them to work with me individually throughout the day. In turn, they begin to care for me as well. In reality, my connection with each student doesn't start the year that they are placed in my classroom. Relationships are forged over time by interacting in the hallway, at recess, and walking into the building in the morning. A simple, "Hello!" or a high five is a great way to show students that you care about children and are happy to be a teacher. By the time a child is assigned to my classroom, I've already begun to lay a foundation for a successful school year. When children feel happy and safe at school, they're willing to work hard for their teachers. And hard-working students are what it's going to take to create a successful student-led classroom!

COMMON CONCERNS ABOUT STUDENT-LED CLASSROOMS

"You must be the change you wish to see in the world."

—Mahatma Gandhi

The decision to transition to a student-led classroom can be a challenging one. Worries about managing a chaotic classroom, adding more work to an already busy schedule, or watching students' grades slip can make the shift seem risky. In my experience, switching to a student-led classroom has eliminated many more challenges than it's created. If you believe students should be empowered and have some control over their learning, you and your students can handle any adversity that may come along. After all, handling challenges that arise in a student-led classroom is better than dealing with a lack of motivation, poor behavior, and student apathy any day! Later in this chapter, I'll share a few more of the amazing benefits that result when students are encouraged to collaborate and lead. But first, let's take a look at a few common concerns that keep teachers from unfurling the sails and letting their students take charge of the ship... I mean classroom.

PIRATES DON'T GIVE UP WHEN THE WIND BLOWS THEM OFF COURSE; THEY ADJUST THEIR SAILS AND CONTINUE TOWARD THEIR DESTINATION!

Most of the reasons and fears that cause teachers to hesitate to create student-led classrooms are easily addressed and dispelled. In fact, once you decide to embrace a new way of teaching that will have profound effects on your students, success is only a matter of staying the course. And yes, you will have some setbacks along the way. They're to be expected. But the rewards outweigh the risks. Remember: Pirates don't give up when the wind blows them off course; they adjust their sails and continue toward their destination!

I've heard from many teachers who want to create a better learning experience for their students but find this unfamiliar territory somewhat scary. If you are wary of creating a student-led classroom, the next few pages are specifically for you. I hope the encouragement and real-life insights here give you the confidence you need to make the change. And if you are already excited about creating a student-led classroom, then the tips and tricks included in this section will help you make the shift sooner rather than later.

CONCERN: "I'm worried about giving up control to my students."

It's hard to relinquish control. But let me tell you a little secret: You're not really giving it up! Every one of my students knows that, ultimately, my say is final. I simply choose not to interfere with most of their decisions. Even when a decision is sure to lead us in the wrong direction, I usually choose to follow it through! I want them to learn from their mistakes! Of course, sometimes we don't have time for that, and at those times I might intervene.

You should see my students' faces when the group decides to take a big risk! They look at me to see if I appear to be scared or concerned; but I have a pretty good poker face! I might be thinking, "Oh, this won't work!" But my body language and facial expressions are saying, "Let's try it!" It's so important to encourage your students to be risk-takers. Otherwise, they'll be completely content to follow whatever everyone else is doing in life. The last thing I want to do is turn out a bunch of kids who give in to peer pressure!

CONCERN: "I can't do this. I'm definitely going to make a lot of mistakes and fail."

You *will* make mistakes. We all do. You might even make more mistakes than you're used to at first. Whenever I make a mistake in my class, I choose to use it at as a teaching experience. I even point out my mistakes to my students! I want them to know failure is not embarrassing or something that needs to be hidden. Failure and mistakes are an important part of the learning process. Your students need you to model a healthy reaction to failure so they too can handle their mistakes with dignity and class.

CONCERN: "There's just too much at stake. I can't risk this not working."

Here's the good news: If you fail at creating a student-led classroom, you end up with a teacher-led classroom! At least you tried! Your students and administrators will certainly appreciate your efforts, and you will have learned a great deal in the process. *Learning* is the goal. *Any* progress you make toward empowering your students to become active leaders and doers, rather than passive followers who don't know how to think for themselves, will benefit their education.

CONCERN: "This will be too much work. I can't take on another thing right now!"

By definition, students take on most of the responsibility in a student-led classroom. Your job is to explain your expectations and provide students with opportunities to practice their skills. Be supportive and patient when they make mistakes. Remind them (and yourself) that new skills take time to develop. Teaching is hard no matter what we do, but I assure you that empowering your students to run the classroom will eliminate more issues than it creates.

CONCERN: "I'm overwhelmed. I don't know where to begin!"

Why not start by talking with your class about the direction you'd like things to go? During this discussion, give them the power to interrupt when they have something important that needs to be said. (See "Give Me Five" on page 40.) The power to interrupt the class is the single, most important thing you can do to empower your students to lead.

Provide opportunities for your students to lead the class and one another. Give lots of feedback and spend time reflecting on your progress as a class. Those changes alone are enough to create dramatic differences. You'll discover many ideas in the coming chapters that can be easily implemented in your classroom.

CONCERN: "But, won't my room get loud?"

Absolutely! Think of it as the sound of productivity. My room is definitely one of the louder classes in the school. And that's okay with me, because when I walk around, I see that my students are *actively engaged in learning.* They're collaborating and problem-solving. Sometimes that requires making a little noise! (Occasionally, a student will interrupt the class and announce, "It's getting too loud. I can't even hear my partner!" When that happens, I comment that these conversations are productive noise. I suggest they move around the room to find a quieter location to work, rather than try to eliminate any of the important discussions.)

Because I have loud, active, motivated students, what I don't have are sleepy, zoned-out children. I don't have kids who want to sneak away to the bathroom for a break. I don't have kids checking their phones or playing games online. Instead, my kids work through their recesses and forget that lunch has started because they're excited about what they're doing in class. These are the signs of engaged, motivated youngsters who enjoy learning, not for a grade or for a reward, but because it's *fun*.

CONCERN: "There's no time for all of this. There's just too much to do."

I get questions from teachers and administrators every year about how we fit so much into our schedule. "Show me your weekly schedule. What *aren't* you teaching?" they ask. My answer is that we maximize our time-on-task, make transitions efficient, and we integrate subjects.

Careful planning is a huge part of fitting everything in. I spend a lot of time during the summer planning out the school year to make sure all the appropriate subjects are covered and learning goals are met. I also carefully plan out each week. As a result, we waste very little time. Lessons are given only the time they need (not more), and units that share common factors are often combined.

IN A TEACHER-LED CLASSROOM THE WHOLE CLASS HAS TO STOP WHAT THEY'RE DOING WHEN THE TEACHER IS DISTRACTED.

For example, I typically don't use textbooks or tests in my class (math is an exception), but I do teach a government unit with a student-friendly textbook. I have integrated content-area reading skills, note-taking, study, and test-taking skills into the unit to equip my students for their future schooling. It is a natural opportunity to combine several skills into one unit. Students understand all the concepts better because nothing is taught in isolation. Plus, we save time by merging the lessons!

Continuous flow is another time-saving benefit of a student-led classroom. Think about how much time is lost each day to interruptions. You might have to pause to deal with a discipline issue or stop to fix technology that isn't working. Clarifying directions and answering questions take time. Occasionally, you might have to pause your instruction to answer a phone call or talk to someone who has stopped by your room. No matter the reason, in a teacher-led classroom the whole class has to stop what they're doing when the teacher is distracted.

Imagine those inevitable situations happening while students are working in small groups or partnerships. Do they have to stop what they're doing when you answer the phone? Do they lose their concentration when you help a student who has a question? Are they forced to wait while you talk to Mr. Lamich who just walked in? No! Their learning continues and time on-task is maximized. We're talking about dozens of hours of learning time gained each year. *That's how I fit it all in!*

Anticipation is one final factor that keeps my class focused. My students are always looking forward to what comes next on our schedule, because they direct the class to transition to the next activity (even when the activity is new to them). No more running over time and having to cancel the next activity. With so little downtime, behavior problems and off-task behavior rarely happen. Active students have far fewer opportunities to misbehave.

CONCERN: "I can't fit it all into our curriculum. We'll never get through everything."

This is not "another thing." Nor does it require a new set of lessons. It's about how your students learn. You can establish a student-led classroom while teaching your current lessons. Begin by tweaking the lessons so that students take a more active role while you assume a more passive role. When you're ready, you can add lessons that are naturally more student-led.

CONCERN: "My students can't do this."

Start small. Give your students simple jobs. Get your students to do a single task on their own without a reminder from you. Slowly build in more responsibilities. In my school, even the first and second grade teachers use these tactics to encourage students to take ownership of their learning—and it works! Impress upon your students the importance of awareness. Empower them to make decisions. They will make mistakes along the way, but imagine the skills they'll learn and be able to apply in future years.

I beg you to have high expectations for your students. Too often, we are the ones making excuses and preventing our students from stepping up to challenges. We need to be the ones providing them with opportunities to struggle. We need to be helping them handle the failures and setbacks and telling them that we're proud of them for being risk-takers. We need to stop lowering the bar and expecting the worst. Trust that your students can do this. They will make you proud!

CONCERN: "I don't want chaos! I have students who will ruin it for the class."

Maybe you're thinking, "But I have Jimmy and Billy and Amanda in my class this year, and they'll mess it up for everyone!" Believe me, I understand your concern. Some students seem to have a knack for disruption. However, I've discovered that even the most troubled students fare amazingly well in a student-led environment. They may start the school year acting a little silly or showing no desire to participate, but with regular feedback and short conversations about the importance of respecting the power I've given them, they improve quickly! In fact, that power is often the *reason* they succeed. After all, power and attention are the two main reasons students misbehave. Empowering students to lead the classroom gives them both.

I'm not the only one who has recognized the impact of this teaching style. During the past fifteen years, I've received dozens of positive comments from substitute teachers after they've spent the day with my students. Read a few of their observations:

> *"Students were wonderful; we had no problems at all. They are so independent!"*

> *"You have a great group of students. They are very proud of their room and how they run it. Everything went smoothly."*

> *"Overall, it was a great day! You have a nice group of students—very focused!"*

> *"You have a wonderful group of kids; they are so kind and helpful. I had a wonderful morning working with them!"*

> *"Great day! Really great class! They rate a perfect score!"*

> *"The class was very good and a pleasure to teach. Very respectful of each other and did the work that was requested. They were also very helpful."*

"You have a very nice group! They are polite, responsible, hardworking, and really seem to respect each other!"

"Your students and their interactions with each other were very impressive."

To me, these comments offer evidence that, regardless of the mix of students through the years, they've all been able to step up to the challenge of running our student-led classroom. Even my most challenging students have excelled when empowered and entrusted to lead.

CONCERN: "I have shy and introverted students who will feel uncomfortable."

Each year, children of all personality types come into my classroom. Some are outgoing, some are mischievous, some are creative, and some are introverted. It's a misconception that shy and introverted children cannot become strong leaders. In a classroom that values leadership of all kinds, introverted children often discover that they can lead by example and collaborate with others in partnerships.

All personality types can succeed in a student-led environment, provided that a few factors are true.

1. Teachers must express the importance of taking risks and being strong leaders, despite reservations.

2. Teachers must give gentle nudges and assist students who feel reluctant to lead. No pressure, just encouragement.

3. Parents should be asked to be supportive of this style of learning even (or perhaps especially) if their child has reservations about being a leader. When parents and teachers calmly encourage children to participate in the classroom's operation, students are more likely to take necessary risks.

4. Neither teachers nor parents should try to change a child's personality type. Students can remain shy and reserved and still be successful in our classroom environment. They just need to become comfortable with the way the classroom runs. Once they are comfortable, they will take more chances. Although they may never be the most vocal students, they will become valuable leaders within their small groups.

5. Finally, teachers must model desired behavior, especially in response to mistakes. When you overreact, students overreact. When you calmly explain a better way to do something, students will mimic that as well.

IT'S BETTER TO ASK FOR FORGIVENESS THAN PERMISSION. IT'S DIFFICULT TO ARGUE WITH POSITIVE RESULTS.

CONCERN: "Parents and administrators won't like it."

Can you imagine what people must think when they walk into my student-led classroom for the first time? I might be sitting at a table with four students, watching and participating in a discussion, while twenty-three other students are doing dozens of different things with virtually no supervision.

How might parents feel? What will my principal say?

If they spend a few minutes watching each student, they will notice that nearly everyone is focused, on-task, and happy—because their peers wouldn't have it any other way! Students get so much done when they know what to do, are given enjoyable tasks, have the time and space to do their work, and are empowered to make their own decisions!

Many parents have told me that fifth grade was the year their children started liking school or reading or working with others.

They came home and excitedly talked about what they were doing in school and shared photos from our online Daily Photo Journal. Suddenly, it was easy to get their children up and off to school in the morning because they looked forward to something they were doing in class. I can't imagine any parent having an issue with easier mornings and happy, enthusiastic children, can you?

My building administrators appreciate that the students run our day. They see increased confidence in these students, as well as a deep respect for their peers. They understand that conversation between all students is vital to our collaborative environment and an important part of twenty-first century learning.

If you're worried about how your administrators or students' parents will react, remember: It's better to ask for forgiveness than permission. It's difficult to argue with positive results.

CONCERN: "My way of teaching has worked for years. I don't need to change."

I hope you will keep an open mind about implementing a student-led classroom because times have changed. Access to technology and other resources have inspired innovation in my classroom in the past few years—I can't imagine teaching the way I used to teach!

But the changes extend far beyond technology. Children are different; the world is different.

My most recent philosophical and pedagogical changes have reinvigorated me and made me a much better teacher than I was before. Although I am working harder than I ever have before, the work feels undeniably valuable and worth the investment of time and effort. Spending hours of my free time grading, copying, and creating tests just didn't feel like time well spent. Now, I spend my time planning lessons and units that inspire my students, connecting with teachers and students around the globe, and reading books and articles about better ways to teach.

Teaching has remained relatively unchanged over the centuries in most parts of the world, but that doesn't mean those old methods are the best ways to teach and learn! I believe children deserve to have a voice in their education. They shouldn't have to sit all day long and learn facts and concepts that a handful of teachers deemed important ages ago.

Sure, change can be scary, but it can also be exciting! What you'll see in your students as they take charge of their education and learn to lead themselves and one another will thrill you. If you're brave enough to embark on this adventure with your class, you'll (re)discover the truth that children learn best when they are encouraged and empowered to explore their passions and curiosities. Working alongside you and their peers, your students will realize, perhaps for the first time, that learning can be fun!

"I think it's important in this day and age, to be a self-starter. Taking responsibility for yourself is something that is learned. Kids are not born with this ability. Someone, typically parents in the past, has to raise children to be responsible, contributing members of society. But why should it stop there? This lesson should come from all directions: family, school, community, church, and more. And being a 'leader' is not just about aspiring to be a CEO of a *Fortune* 500 company. It's more about leading your own life and setting examples for others."

—*Mary DeMaria, Parent*

EXPERIENCE THE BENEFITS OF A STUDENT-LED CLASSROOM

Transitioning to a student-led classroom can have a tremendous impact on the educational experience for both students and teachers in so many ways. Students retain more of what they learn, due to their active participation in the learning process, as well as their continuous feedback from both the teacher and their peers. Teachers are afforded daily opportunities to observe and give students feedback throughout the learning process, which improves their craft and helps them perform stronger on their annual reviews.

INCREASED RETENTION

One of the many reasons I hope you will create a student-led classroom is because active learning has been proven to be more effective than passive learning when measuring academic gains.

Confucius observed two-and-a-half millennia ago that people learn best through experience. He said, "I hear and I forget. I see and I remember. I do and I understand."

All veteran teachers have taught units before, only to test their students and discover that nearly the entire class struggled. Our first instinct is to be upset with the students for not focusing, studying, or trying hard enough. But the reality is that the way we teach a subject impacts how much students can learn. Asking them to passively learn by listening to lectures and reading content in textbooks is not efficient or effective for most children.

Children learn best by doing, by questioning, and by figuring out solutions on their own. In this day and age when technology enables our students to find answers to their questions in seconds, we can serve them better by teaching them to ask better questions and empowering them to discover the answers themselves. They may even learn that some questions have more than one right answer.

CHILDREN LEARN BEST BY DOING, BY QUESTIONING, AND BY FIGURING OUT SOLUTIONS ON THEIR OWN.

When students are given the responsibility of acquiring knowledge through research, communication, and problem-solving, teachers no longer need to be the sole purveyors of information. More *doing* on the students' part is necessary if we hope to get them to transfer their skills to real situations. Creating successful, independent thinkers is, after all, one of the main purposes of education!

CONE OF LEARNING

According to Edgar Dale's Cone of Learning[1], students only learn 10 percent of what they read, 20 percent of what they hear being told to them, 30 percent of what they see in presentations and visuals, and 50 percent of what they hear *and* see.

Even for the most attentive of learners, passive learning makes retention of information difficult. Dale suggests that active learning (e.g. participating in a discussion with peers, speaking about a topic, etc.) can lead to 70 percent retention! Actively participating and choosing which words to say when speaking increases the chances of permanent learning. Better yet, when students both say and do something like a dramatic presentation, simulating a real experience, or *leading the class*, they remember 90 percent of that information and can apply it to new situations.

Now imagine the amount of learning that will happen when your students participate in a student-led classroom! They're learning while developing other important skills, such as collaboration, leadership, self-direction, grit, and problem-solving, among dozens of others. Authentic, long-term learning of content and life skills happens in a student-led classroom because students are allowed to think for themselves and work together to find solutions to their problems.

MORE TIME FOR FEEDBACK

Student-led classrooms allow teachers the time to give immediate, personalized feedback to students. Now, I don't suggest leaving the classroom to work one-on-one with each student while the rest of the class works. That's a recipe for disaster! Students need regular supervision and they need to believe you are an active participant in each activity. But you *can and should* walk around while students work and have short conversations with individual students, offer guidance, and ask thought-provoking questions to help them improve their work. Then, make another pass around the room. It's important to be omnipresent, but eventually students will just assume that you are around, even when you are working with a student in the corner of the room.

ACTIVELY PARTICIPATING AND CHOOSING WHICH WORDS TO SAY WHEN SPEAKING INCREASE THE CHANCES OF PERMANENT LEARNING.

Since you have the time to observe, you will be able to spot struggling students and provide feedback quickly to re-direct them before they become frustrated. At the beginning of the year, when I know students may be sensitive to struggling, I will ask a neighbor who clearly understands the task to explain it or show it to me while I stand over them and watch. I will make sure that the struggling students are paying attention and encourage them to try it next. This slowly builds their confidence and helps them understand that even though we all have different background knowledge, we'll all get to the same place eventually with practice.

Later in the year, I tend to encourage my struggling students to work with a nearby peer until they get the hang of whatever they're trying to do. Since they understand that improvement is the goal, they don't take offense or become embarrassed. Reinforcing collaboration and critical thinking (instead of solving the problem myself) instills the belief that students can and should rely on one another to accomplish tasks rather than look to the teacher for answers. I am a resource, but I don't want to be first on the list.

TEACHER EVALUATION

Another benefit of creating a student-led classroom comes from a completely extrinsic source. Teacher evaluation seems to be headed in that direction. Our district, and hundreds of others, have recently adopted Charlotte Danielson's model for teacher evaluation[2]. To achieve the highest rating, teachers need to empower their students to lead the show!

Administrators across the country are being trained to look for specific teacher behaviors. Additionally, teachers are being evaluated on how they have (or have not) empowered their students. Here are some behaviors administrators are looking for with regard to the *Classroom Environment:*

- Students demonstrate genuine caring for one another and monitor one another's treatment of peers, correcting classmates respectfully when needed.
- Students demonstrate through their active participation, curiosity, and taking initiative that they value the importance of the content.
- Students demonstrate attention to detail and take obvious pride in their work, initiating improvements in it by, for example, revising drafts on their own or helping peers.

- Transitions are seamless, with students assuming responsibility in ensuring their efficient operation.
- Routines for handling materials and supplies are seamless, with students assuming some responsibility for smooth operation.
- Systems for performing non-instructional duties are well-established, with students assuming considerable responsibility for efficient operation.
- Monitoring by teacher is subtle and preventive. Students monitor their own and their peers' behaviors, correcting one another respectfully.
- The classroom is safe, and students themselves ensure that all learning is equally accessible to all students.
- Both teacher and students use physical resources easily and skillfully, and students adjust the furniture to advance their learning.

Administrators are also looking to see that teachers have empowered their students to do actions, such as the following, with regard to *Instruction:*

- Teacher's explanation of content is imaginative and connects with students' knowledge and experience. Students contribute to explaining concepts to their peers.

EXPLAINING CONCEPTS

- Students assume considerable responsibility for the success of the discussion, initiating topics and making unsolicited contributions.
- Students themselves ensure that all voices are heard in the discussion.

31

- All students are cognitively engaged in the activities and assignments in their exploration of content. Students initiate or adapt activities and projects to enhance their understanding.

- Instructional groups are productive and fully appropriate to the students or to the instructional purposes of the lesson. Students take the initiative to influence the formation or adjustment of instructional groups.

- Instructional materials and resources are suitable to the instructional purposes and engage students mentally. Students initiate the choice, adaptation, or creation of materials to enhance their learning.

- Students are fully aware of the criteria and performance standards by which their work will be evaluated and have contributed to the development of the criteria.

- Teacher's feedback to students is timely and of consistently high quality, and students make use of their feedback in their learning.

- Students not only frequently assess and monitor the quality of their own work against the assessment criteria and performance standards but also make active use of that information in their learning.

As you can see, quite a few performance descriptors rely on teachers to create an environment where students lead themselves and their peers without reliance on the teacher. The reality is that creating a student-led classroom is not only good for your students; it can benefit your teaching career as well!

I am committed to providing the best possible learning environment for my students, and I believe you are reading this book because you have that same dedication. That's good, because your students need you! Take a risk. Be open to change and to a new, student-led approach to teaching. The personal and academic growth you'll see in your students and the rewards you'll experience as a teaching professional far outweigh the effort. I promise.

RESOURCES

---

[1] Edgar Dale's Cone of Learning—
http://www.biztechreport.com/images/useyourhead.jpg

[2] *Implementing the Framework for Teaching in Enhancing Professional Practice*, Heinle ELT, ©2009

SECTION 2

LEARN LIKE A PIRATE

PROMOTING STUDENT LEADERSHIP IN THE CLASSROOM REQUIRES:

PEER COLLABORATION

IMPROVEMENT FOCUS VS. GRADE FOCUS

RESPONSIBILITY

ACTIVE LEARNING

TWENTY-FIRST CENTURY SKILLS FOCUS

EMPOWERMENT

Peer Collaboration

"People who work together will win, whether it be against complex football defenses or the problems of modern society."
—Vince Lombardi

As I sit here writing, I'm reminded of just how important collaboration is to me. After all, I'm writing independently, or so it seems. In reality, by the time you read *Learn Like a Pirate*, hundreds if not thousands of people will have influenced its message. Obviously, my publisher and my editor gave their input (Thanks, you guys!), but they are only a few among many. Through the years, I have been influenced as an educator by the books I've read, like *Teach Like a PIRATE* by Dave Burgess, *The Passion-Driven Classroom* by Angela Maiers, *Comprehension & Collaboration* by Stephanie Harvey and Harvey Daniels, and so many more. My professional learning network (PLN), a growing group of people who constantly challenge me to think differently about things I *thought* made sense, have left their marks. Students and co-workers, who have entered and exited my life during the past sixteen years, have helped shape my thinking and teaching practices. And every interaction I've had with my parents, sister, niece, and nephew has enhanced and continues to refine the way I think and the way I behave. Although I spent most of my time writing this book alone, collaboration has been an integral part of this entire experience.

TEACHING
COLLABORATION

Similarly, collaboration is the cornerstone of a student-led classroom. Every new school year, I tell my students, "Two brains are better than one!" And I mean it! Collaboration allows us to know more than we are capable of knowing by ourselves. Collaboration involves thinking about other people's ideas and synthesizing them with our own. True collaboration causes us to think differently, access information that otherwise would have been missed or ignored, and combine ideas to come up with solutions to problems.

In a classroom devoid of collaboration, cliques form, animosity breeds, and students isolate themselves. Individual needs come before the needs of the class. Some students try hard to be the best, while others lose interest and stop trying. And where social hierarchies exist and lack of respect prevails, student-led classrooms fail because children refuse to be led.

WE'RE IN THIS TOGETHER

As you can see, it's imperative for teachers to work hard to immediately foster and then maintain a sense of community in the classroom. From the first day of school on, I want my students to know *we're not just a class; we're a crew! We're in this together!* I tend to look at my classroom as a cross between a close-knit family and a forward-thinking company. As a *family*, we look out for and help one another. Even when we disagree and argue, we show one another respect and quickly forgive and forget. Bullying or teasing from students outside our classroom rarely affects students in our classroom because we have one another's backs—no one stands alone. As a *company*, we know every team member is important. We rely on one another as we work together. Our company has a *revisionist* mentality, rather than a completion mentality. We're not a boring factory, cranking out widgets; we are an innovative organization working together to create something amazing.

IF YOU WANT TO CREATE A STUDENT-LED CLASSROOM, SET THE STAGE BY ESTABLISHING A COLLABORATIVE COMMUNITY.

Which companies perform better? Companies where bosses micro-manage their employees? Or those at which bosses give clear direction, offer consistent support and feedback, and maintain high expectations? I bet you already know my answer. In our classroom, I intentionally choose not to micro-manage. Instead, we discuss expectations together. I provide immediate feedback and support when necessary, but there are no one-way conversations in my classroom. Everyone has a voice and is encouraged to share his or her thoughts. My "employees" work with autonomy to get things done their way because I know my way isn't the only way. In this collaborative classroom community, students begin to feel respected enough to give others directions, confident enough to purposely focus others' attention on themselves, and safe enough to take chances.

If you want to create a student-led classroom, set the stage by establishing a collaborative community—that combination of family and company. Then, use the strategies you'll find throughout this book. Be intentional about handing over control. Teach students the differences and value of active and passive leadership. Set up a classroom layout that encourages participation. Get students working in partnerships quickly. After all, a crew that works together wins together!

"GIVE ME FIVE"—
EMPOWER STUDENTS TO LEAD

"Give me five!"

Those three little words give my students the power they need to lead. When a student shouts, "Give me five! Give me five!" everyone in the classroom (including the teacher) stops what they are doing, faces the speaker, and listens intently to their message.

Teachers have used "Give Me Five" for years as a way to get their class's attention, usually to quiet it down. By giving this privilege to your students, they have the single, most powerful tool to be able to lead the classroom—the power to interrupt so they can lead and direct their peers. Students won't listen to one another if they don't have any power! But they know the simple command of, "Give Me Five!" will get the attention of the whole class, including the teacher ("Give Me Fives" are one of many ways to empower your students to lead. You'll find several other strategies in the "Empowerment" chapter, but we use this particular tool so frequently in my class, I felt it was important to introduce it early in the book!)

"The type of classroom setting that Paul Solarz creates has laid groundwork for our son as he moves on to middle school and high school, where students are expected to be much more independent and self-directed. His teaching approach comes at a perfect time for elementary students, especially fifth grade boys who are easily distracted at this age.

"Students helped each other on various levels and learned how teamwork can stimulate problem solving. As their future school careers and their lives outside the classroom involve working with others, this student-led environment better prepares students for what's ahead of them.

"Quite simply, Paul Solarz empowers students to be proactive about learning with interactive and incentive-based tasks. Our son was truly motivated by this type of classroom atmosphere. We feel that this year, more than any other in his elementary career, has prepared him for the challenges that lie ahead."

—*Stacy and John Stapleton, Parents*

HELP IT GROW

For the first few weeks, express your appreciation for students who use "Give Me Fives" in the correct context and politely provide feedback for those using it incorrectly. A huge learning curve exists when students begin to take control of their classroom. Whenever opportunities are missed for a "Give Me Five," point them out to the whole class and model how it could have been done. They'll catch on!

EXAMPLES OF HOW STUDENTS USE "GIVE ME FIVES" IN OUR CLASSROOM:

1. I don't watch the clock throughout the day, but I do post a schedule with exact transition times on it. I *expect* my students to let the others and me know when we're getting close to a transition time (e.g. a five-minute warning) and when it's time to actually transition (e.g. "Time to transition for Math!"). If we go over time, I remind them that it is *their* responsibility to ensure that we transition on time.

2. If a student has a polite suggestion for how to improve the class's behavior at a given time, he or she can suggest it. I model this. Whenever students are off-task, for example, staring at the snow out the window instead of reading along during shared reading, I say, "Give me five!" and proceed to identify the behavior, explain what I expect, and request that everyone try their best! I'll say something like, "I think some of us might be a bit off-task and maybe we should try to re-focus." Or, "We are presenting tomorrow, so maybe it's time to start writing if you haven't started already."

3. One of the most common "Give Me Five" uses is to make a suggestion for improving a task we are working on. Our class record for moving seats is one minute, eight seconds. My students like to problem-solve ways of beating that class record. "Why don't we try to move our desks clockwise and stay out of the middle, instead of everyone just pushing them everywhere? It might help us break the class record!"

4. Students can use "Give Me Fives" to ask the whole class a question when no one knows the answer. (e.g. "I've already asked the people at my table, 'Which website were we supposed to start with?'") By asking the class, instead of waiting for me to come to them, they get a quick response, and I remain free to observe and give feedback.

5. "Give Me Fives" can be an offer to demonstrate a skill that others might need in the future. For example, "I'm showing Jimmy how to make a screencast, if anyone else would like to learn!" Or, "I just learned how to change the font color and would be happy to share it with anyone who wants to see it."

"Give Me Fives" can be used for dozens of other purposes. As you encourage students to take control in the classroom, they will discover new ways to use this important tool.

TEACHING STUDENTS TO USE THEIR POWER WISELY

The power to interrupt the class is one of the most important aspects of a student-led classroom. Of course, this power could be dangerous if students aren't taught to harness it properly. After all, "with great power comes great responsibility!" I invest a lot of time at the beginning of the school year teaching my students about the importance of respecting the "Give Me Five" signal. We have a discussion about the importance of not abusing the privilege of "Give Me Fives." I warn them about prior students who have mockingly said, "Give me three" or "Give me ten," and how that doesn't respect the privilege or me. We talk about the importance of not overusing the privilege and which situations might not need a "Give Me Five." I also let them know "Give Me Fives" are not allowed in specials (Art, Music, PE) and are limited with substitutes to one or two per person for the day.

Whenever someone ignores the call, I provide immediate feedback to correct the behavior and carefully explain the importance of taking it seriously, out of respect to the student, as well as to me. It's so important that students show respect for the child who is taking the risk of speaking in front of the group. If students don't develop this respect, "Give Me Five" won't work.

Like you, I've had a few bossy students who love to control others, as well as those that enjoy the spotlight. But taking care of these individual cases is very easy with one-on-one conversations about my expectations and temporary restrictions from using a "Give Me Five" until improvement is shown. Don't forget, when a student shouts, "Give me five!," your eyes are focused on that student. It's the perfect opportunity to use the power of the teacher's stare if he or she isn't appropriately respecting the privilege.

One of the hardest things for teachers, with regard to "Give Me Fives," is that students occasionally interrupt at inopportune times. For example, students might shout, "Give me five!" when you are about to talk to the class, or when everyone is silently working or taking a test, or when you are Skyping with another class from around the world. Rather than get frustrated or embarrassed, be proud that they took the risk to lead the class. Try hard not to discourage them from taking initiative. Because they know "Give Me Fives" are an important privilege, they really *want* to use it right. When I offer feedback, they almost always apologize if they think they've interrupted me. They almost always say something really important when it's during a test. (Usually it's something I would have forgotten about, so they are bailing me out!) And the other class we are Skyping is almost always impressed by my students' leadership.

PROVIDING AMPLE OPPORTUNITY FOR STUDENT LEADERSHIP

Giving students the power to interrupt the class takes you only halfway toward empowering your students. You also have to provide them with opportunities to use this power!

> # STUDENTS LEAD WHEN THEY BELIEVE THE TEACHER WOULD APPRECIATE THEIR HELP, NOT WHEN THE TEACHER IS COMPLETELY IN CHARGE.

Imagine a classroom where the teacher is always on stage and the students are always in their seats. Or envision a classroom where students are expected to silently complete worksheets at their desks. How comfortable are students going to feel about leading in these kinds of environments?

If a teacher is constantly teaching from the front, most students will assume that the teacher has everything under control and may only need a reminder when the class period is close to ending. When teachers lead, students don't easily see how they can help. Aside from limited opportunities for leadership, what student is going to feel comfortable using a "Give Me Five" in a silent classroom?

Students lead when they believe the teacher would appreciate their help, not when the teacher is completely in charge. To get my students involved, I tell them how much I need them to help with the management of our class. I tell them that I rarely look at the clock, I rarely remember what we're doing next, I rarely know when we need the computer cart, etc. By putting those responsibilities on my entire class, I'm giving everyone opportunities to step up and become leaders. I continue to present requests all year long to let students know what I need them to do for me and their peers: "Please make sure that everyone in your group understands what to do before you begin." "Please check your neighbor's paper to see if the first four steps are done. If not, please help him or her catch up."

In my classroom, I have chosen to delegate nearly every responsibility for our classroom's operation to the students as a collective whole. That doesn't mean I never do those tasks, but that we share the responsibilities equally. For example, if I have some free time, I will occasionally get the computer cart while the class is at recess. If I'm closer to the phone than my students are, I'll answer it. I will occasionally set up the morning video announcements before they walk into the classroom if I'm ready to start my day and have no one with me for Homework Club. But my students know that, if something isn't done, someone needs to do it. Most importantly, they understand that the responsibility falls on the students, not the teacher.

"Learning begins in school and continues throughout life. In school, a teacher's job is to train the student, which the student will one day apply to a career. Having students 'take charge,' gives them the feel of how the real world works."

—*Jeanine Bogdanovski, Parent*

ENCOURAGE ACTIVE AND PASSIVE LEADERSHIP

At the end of each day, my students collaboratively set one class goal for the next day. Someone needs to get the easel. Someone needs to write down the goal. And everyone should have input setting the goal. At the end of the school year, this daily process is smooth and exciting. But this scene on the first day (even the first few days) of school is… chaotic.

Let's take a look at what's happened so far on that first day of school. I start the day by explaining that this class might look a little different than what they've experienced in previous years. I tell my students that they will get to own their learning and be in control of our classroom. I set the expectation for the class taking collective responsibility for transitioning between subjects, transporting the computer cart, solving one another's problems, and ensuring that our day runs smoothly. I also let them know I will do my best to give them all the power, directions, and knowledge they need in order to be successful at this endeavor. That being said, I make sure they understand the success of our classroom is the responsibility of the entire class, not specific individuals. Everyone shares the work.

I also tell them that my role as teacher might seem different as well. Instead of spending most of my time in front of the class, my goal is to get to the point where I spend most of my time walking around the room, observing and giving feedback. I explain that, for this to happen, I need my students to become good at listening to directions, following those directions carefully, and working with each other to get tasks done.

By the end of the day, my students begin to grasp what this new power and responsibility mean—at least in theory. And then comes the time to set our goals for the next day. I don't assign the job of getting the chart paper and easel; I just let the students figure it out on their own. So, on that first day, there are always a few kids racing to get the easel, while others argue about who will get to write the goal on the chart paper. And without fail, at least a few try to dominate the class when determining what to write down for the day.

I told you. Chaos!

Instead of getting upset by this crazy scene (and instead of just assigning a new job, which would easily solve the problem), I turn it into a teachable moment. First, I remind my students about the importance of using the conflict management strategies we discussed earlier that same day. (See page 56.) Then, I talk with them about the difference between active leadership and passive leadership.

Active leadership is shown when someone speaks to or directs others and requests that others follow suit. It's when someone actively tries to influence others' behavior. Passive leadership, on the other hand, happens when students lead by example or choose to follow the students who are demonstrating active leadership. Passive leadership shows respect while encouraging others to follow suit.

I explain that the situation with getting the chart paper and writing our goal called for passive leadership. The moment screamed, "Appreciate that others want to be an active leader. You will get your turn another time!" Passive leadership can be hard for some children, especially those who enjoy being in control or love attention. Other children are naturals at it because they appreciate that others are taking charge and not relying on them to lead the troops.

A few days later, one of my students (I still don't know who) created a system where students sign up to be in charge of the easel and writing down our goal. They now take turns every day and have done an outstanding job with it! Students need opportunities like these to problem solve and think creatively.

It's extremely important for teachers to encourage students to be both active *and* passive leaders. There are times that I wished my students would step up their leadership skills and there are times when I wish they would back off a bit. Each situation provides an opportunity to guide them toward becoming active and passive leaders.

In addition to teaching about passive leadership, I make sure to teach my students how to advocate for themselves when they disagree with an active leader. When someone is clearly abusing their powers and causing others to lose focus, it's important that others step in and re-direct. When a student leader is taking the group down the wrong path but doesn't realize it, it's time for a passive leader to step in and politely suggest an alternative. When there are multiple correct ways to do something and a student disagrees with the leader, I teach them to share their thoughts respectfully, but be content to do things in a new way, depending on what the group decides to do.

PROVIDE SPACES THAT ENCOURAGE LEARNING

Classroom layout has recently been a hot topic of discussion on social media. It seems everyone is buying those really cool chairs on wheels with desktops that push out. I love those things! Unfortunately, I don't have the money for fancy desks and chairs, and, to be honest, I'm not sure my students need them. When considering what my students really needed with regard to furniture, I discovered that we had the perfect combination of items in our school already. (You probably do, too!)

Here are my classroom's basic space and furniture needs:

- A place to store materials,
- Lots of places to work for various purposes,
- Seating arrangements that encourage collaboration, discussion, and comfort without distraction,
- A "stage" for direct instruction,
- A floor where we can sit and conduct classroom meetings,
- Tables for small group interactions.

The amazing thing is, when I analyzed our needs, I discovered that the only necessary additions were five hexagonal tables. These tables provide space for small groups and partnerships or can be arranged in a circle in the middle of the classroom.

Transforming Classroom

Honestly, the way you use space (or, more importantly, how your students use the space) in your classroom is more significant than the furniture and its arrangement. Be sure to provide areas in and around your classroom that allow for things, such as making recordings, designing posters, or conducting science investigations. And don't worry too much about seating assignments.

GIVING STUDENTS THEIR CHOICE OF WORK SPACE EMPOWERS THEM TO MAKE THEIR OWN DECISIONS AND MONITOR THEIR OWN BEHAVIOR.

Each of my students has a desk with his or her name tag on it, but that doesn't mean they have to spend much time sitting there. My students are only required to sit at their desks when I am beginning a direct instruction lesson. As soon as they know what to do and have all necessary materials, they can spread out anywhere in the room to complete their tasks. Of course, many students prefer working at desks, just not always their own! Some students enjoy sitting on over-sized pillows on the floor while working. Others like to sit at tables. Nearly everyone loves to sit in one of our classroom's comfy chairs. If more than one person wants one of those chairs, they play rock-paper-scissors for it. Some may choose to work in our classroom library at the back of the room, while others prefer to use the small work room next door to us. Many students like the vestibule between our two double exit doors, and there's always a few who prefer to spread out in the hallway.

Most days, my students work wherever they choose. (Ya gotta love those kids who work while standing!) They're even free to push tables together or separate them as long, as they put them back when they're done. Giving students their choice of work space, empowers them to make their own decisions and monitor their own behavior (and often the behavior of others). No expensive furniture or complete makeovers required!

ASSIGN PARTNERSHIPS TO IMPROVE INTERACTION

If students are going to thrive in a student-led environment (and in the real-world someday), they must learn how to work with all sorts of people and personality types. Collaboration skills don't just come naturally to children, as I'm sure you know. They must be learned. That's why I rarely allow students to choose their partners. They need to develop the skill of working with people, even when personality conflicts arise. Aside from that, my hope is that they get to know everyone in the classroom. After all, we're a family!

Students quickly learn that they will be working with everyone in the class, not just their friends. Boys and girls work together. Students who never get along work together. Friends get to work together. I've even had twins paired together using the tried and true method for creating random partnerships: pulling Popsicle˚ sticks! That's right! Anytime we need to create partnerships, I pull sticks with each student's name on them from a jar. Now, wait! Please don't close the book! I know there are lots of high-tech ways to do the same thing and this may sound outdated. But I'm just being honest; I still prefer to use the sticks!

For some long-term projects (those that require several weeks to complete), I ensure an equitable mix of talents within each group (heterogeneous grouping) by pulling sticks ahead of time and moving a few around to even out skills and abilities. For other activities, I may prefer a more homogeneous group. I then announce group assignments when introducing the project. It's preferable that a boy or girl is not alone in a group for long-term projects, but for day-to-day activities, being the only boy or girl in a group is fine. That being said, my students will almost always choose to be the only boy or girl in a group if it means they get their first choice in book selection or topic choice. (See "Literature Circles," page 130.)

Random partnerships help build strong student relationships amongst everyone in the room. In addition to adding to the class's sense of community, learning to work with anyone without difficulty is a skill they'll use the rest of their lives.

Use Responsibility Partners to Raise the Bar

Occasionally, students are asked to create individual final products. If the task is difficult or I know students will need to collaborate to be successful, I pair them with a "Responsibility Partner."

As with partnerships and small groups, Responsibility Partners can be chosen at random using the aforementioned sticks. Responsibility Partners sit together and bounce ideas off of each other but still come up with their own products using their own ideas. They check in regularly with one another to make sure they each understand the assignment and required tasks, and they confer with one another whenever they have questions. They also hold one another accountable for completing all the steps correctly. This strategy works exceptionally well for creative projects and writing, as well as for math and content-area reading that is not teacher-led.

Responsibility Partners are an extremely important component of classroom operation. When we work with another person, we are able to bounce ideas off of each other and ask each other questions. When we work collaboratively, we combine our knowledge, skills, and direction-following ability and are more likely to be successful.

RESPONSIBILITY PARTNERS IN ACTION

Recently, I showed my students a video of a real-life Rube Goldberg project. After sharing some additional examples in print, I gave them directions for designing their own. Because each student was to create their own diagram and drawing, they were assigned a Responsibility Partner. This allowed them to work independently on their own projects, and, at the same time, collaborate with their peer(s). The results were impressive and each project was improved because students were there to encourage and push one another's creative capacity.

Working together, even on independent activities, improves our chances of learning new things and successfully completing tasks— as long as the partners take the time to work with each other.

When introducing the concept of Responsibility Partners to students, it's important to explain the value of this relationship as well as the importance of each person's role as a partner. Students need to understand that partners share responsibility for one another. When one partner is off-task, they are both responsible. When one partner skips a direction, they are both responsible. When one partner is confused but won't ask questions, they are both responsible. Therefore, it's imperative that they check in on each other's progress regularly. Students also need to be equipped with strategies for redirecting their partners if necessary. These strategies could include:

1. *Asking their partners to do crossovers.* Crossovers provide a brain break when children (or adults) get a bit tired or worn out. Crossovers or cross-lateral movements are those in which your arms or legs cross over the midline from one side of the body to the other. Eric Jensen explains in his book *Teaching with the Brain in Mind* that crossover movements can "force both brain hemispheres to 'talk' to each other better." These simple movements reinvigorate children, which makes learning easier for them.

2. *Asking their partners if they think they need a break to get a drink of water.* That usually gets them to realize they are off-task and they usually just choose to re-focus.

3. *Asking their partners to move to a different location in the classroom to work.* Often, a different perspective and a dif-

ferent chair (and the walk over) can wake up tired minds. Since my students can work anywhere in the classroom, they often choose this option.

4. *Asking their partners if they want to choose a CD to put on.* The right music can have a calming effect. My students are encouraged to play one of my CDs if they think it will help them focus better. (Just keep the sound really low.)

5. *If nothing else works, blame it on the teacher.* I tell my students that they are free to ask their partners to re-focus because Mr. Solarz assigned them as Responsibility Partners. This reminder helps students realize that their partners aren't being annoying; they are just doing their job!

When students share responsibility, they become invested in their peers' success. They work hard to help each other, and they learn to care for everyone in the classroom. In this collaborative setting, students become empathetic and understand that not everyone learns the same way or can focus for the same amount of time. They develop patience and find ways to encourage one another to help maintain focus in the classroom. By assigning Responsibility Partners during independent tasks, you are building up the collaborative atmosphere in your classroom community and helping students form stronger bonds with each other.

TEACHING STRATEGIES FOR DEALING WITH CONFLICT

So, now you have Billy and Joe working together, despite the fact that they never get along. A disagreement breaks out within minutes! What a great opportunity to teach the whole class how to handle conflict and turn this potentially ugly situation into a funny one.

1. Do a "Give Me Five!" to get the class's attention.

2. With a sincere smile on your face, look at Billy and Joe and tell them that you are sooo glad they had a bit of trouble because it allows you this opportunity to teach the whole class how simple it is to get through conflicts in your class. (Embrace the small failures and make them opportunities to learn!)

3. Ask them what the problem was and teach them these strategies for dealing with conflict:

    Rock-Paper-Scissors. I have a T-shirt that I wear to school that says, "Let's settle this like adults! Rock-Paper-Scissors!" You can laugh, but it is a time-honored approach for settling simple disagreements where there has to be a winner (e.g. "I want to be the artist." "No, I want to be the artist!"). Hands down, one of the easiest ways to handle conflict in the classroom is a single round of Rock-Paper-Scissors.

    Compromise. Take ideas from each other and combine them into a plan. (e.g. "I think we should read the article." "But I think we should plan out our steps." "Why don't we plan out our steps, right after we read the article!?") To borrow a phrase from *The Leader in Me* by Stephen Covey: "Think winwin!" Find a way to make both parties happy!

THE LEADER IN ME

Choose Kind. Do what the other person wants to do because it's also a good idea! Our class is not about winning individually, it's about winning as a team. If we win an argument at the expense of our partner, then we've hit a setback (e.g. "Let's flip a coin to see who goes first." "No, I'd rather do rock-paper-scissors." "OK - that works too!") Believe it or not, most of my students are "choosing kind" (to steal a phrase from the book *Wonder* by R.J. Palacio). Because our classroom family is important to everyone, most students are happy to let the other person get their way!

By teaching these strategies to your students early on in the school year, they are more likely to implement them in class (feel free to modify them to work at your grade level, if necessary). If by some miracle you don't have a conflict during the first couple days of the school year, role play a scenario. The earlier you can equip them with positive conflict-management strategies, the better.

REINFORCE THE USE OF CONFLICT-MANAGEMENT STRATEGIES

Every time you overhear or observe a conflict, make it clear that you are aware of the problem (proximity, eye contact, smile, inquisitive look), but you are hoping they will solve it without anyone's help.

If they succeed in getting past the conflict, make sure they know how proud you are of them for using the skills they've learned. Ask if they are willing to share their experience with the class. If so, ask them to do a "Give Me Five" and act out what just happened so others can learn from their experience. If they don't want to or are embarrassed by their behavior, don't push them to share. Many of your students will eventually learn to laugh at their mistakes and gladly share their experiences with the whole group. That's what happens when you provide a caring environment in which improvement, not perfection, is expected.

If students are not successful in getting past the conflict on their own (and no one steps in to help), remind them of the conflict-management strategies and help them move on. You'll be surprised how many students will actually step in to help when they see you observing a disagreement. If their input is offered kindly, make sure that you show your approval of their assistance. Positive feedback reinforces desired behavior for everyone. If the student acts bossy, thank them for trying to help, and model how you prefer they act in the future.

BECAUSE OUR CLASSROOM FAMILY IS IMPORTANT TO EVERYONE, MOST STUDENTS ARE HAPPY TO LET THE OTHER PERSON GET THEIR WAY!

Soon, students will be helping each other solve conflicts whenever they happen. Over time, relationships will grow amongst all of your students, and the disagreements will be more respectful and less common. I'm not exaggerating when I say that I rarely hear arguments between my students the second half of the year. They know how to handle their disagreements, and they respect one another enough to ensure they don't damage their relationships.

CLASSROOM MEETINGS PROMOTE IMMEDIATE CHANGE

Classroom Meetings are a great way to improve the morale, teach social and life skills, and give feedback to the whole class in order to make immediate changes. You may already hold some form of Classroom Meetings. In our classroom, we all sit on the floor together in a cluster. It is mostly teacher-led, but we usually allow time for some discussion at the end. I always have a topic in mind, but rarely use notes to guide me through it, so every Classroom Meeting is a bit different.

Some meetings take only a few minutes and are used to get an important message across in a unique way after other instructional methods have failed. Other meetings can last up to an hour or longer and involve deep introspection and reflection. No matter what, each meeting brings the class closer as a group and improves the students' self-esteem. A classroom filled with happy kids is a classroom that works well together! Therefore, Classroom Meetings always take precedence over whatever we had planned.

EACH MEETING BRINGS THE CLASS CLOSER AS A GROUP AND IMPROVES THE STUDENTS' SELF-ESTEEM

Each class's needs are different. To meet the needs of your individual students, look for problems that could improve if collectively addressed. Below are a few of the topics that have been discussed in my Classroom Meetings through the years. You'll notice that a few of the subjects are covered in books that aren't typically found on a fifth-grade reading list. As in so many other aspects of a student-led classroom, raising your expectations of what kids are capable of can improve *everyone's* experience. (*Note*: Students aren't asked to read the books, but I encourage you to add these important resources to your professional-development library.)

- *The Seven Habits of Highly Effective People* by Stephen Covey
- *The Five Love Languages* (Languages of Appreciation) by Gary Chapman
- Niche Theory (Understanding Birth Order with Relation to Sibling Rivalry)
- The Six Traits of *Character Counts!*
- How to Handle Bullying
- Avoiding Cliques
- Optimism vs. Pessimism
- Introversion vs. Extroversion
- Leading vs. Following
- Right-Brained vs. Left-Brained
- Learning Styles
- Perception vs. Reality
- Hearing vs. Listening
- Active vs. Passive Leadership
- Subjectiveness vs. Objectiveness
- Dealing with Anger and Frustration
- Being a Good Friend
- and so many more...

"Last night my daughter asked me, 'What love language do you speak?' When I probed, she explained that different people share and receive messages in different ways and that it is beneficial to interact with others in a way that they will find most accepting and motivational.

"She's 10.

"I'm 43 and I help teach this team-building concept and collaborative technique to adults—sometimes even management-level employees—in the workplace. Even so, I still have a hard time remembering to adapt my approach to best meet others' needs.

"She learned this concept from Paul Solarz, an exceptional fifth-grade teacher with an unconventional approach to educating children and an extended definition of what a fifth grader needs to know in order to be successful in middle school and beyond.

"Mr. Solarz calls his program 'twenty-first century learning.' In a way the title is a misnomer because it implies a sole emphasis on technology. Although it is true, Mr. Solarz incorporates technology into all that he does, probably more so than in the average classroom; his curriculum extends well beyond iPads, Weebly sites, and Google Docs.

"Mr. Solarz's teachings also go far beyond the basic reading, writing, and 'rithmetic.

And his lessons in character extend well beyond the basic 'five pillars' and the Golden Rule.

"Rather, Mr. Solarz has created a classroom where communication, collaboration, creativity, critical thinking, and curiosity are key. . . where interdependence and interaction breed innovation. . . and where responsibility, risk-taking, and reflection are the new fourth, fifth and sixth 'Rs.'

"My best comparison is that Mr. Solarz's twenty-first century learning is like bringing a private liberal arts college education to the grade school level in that his approach extends beyond the tactical and inspires thoughtful analysis, reflection and questioning.

"His holistic approach and person-centric techniques have led to results that are to be commended. Our daughter managed all her homework and high academic achievement this year with little-to-no parental oversight; she tested ten points higher than she was predicted to on her placement tests, and she is frequently told she is 'wise beyond her years.'

"Having said so, twenty-first century learning was not the only key to our daughter's success this year. Good, old-fashioned love, mentoring, and kindness from a respected leader had a lot to do with it, too. Mr. Solarz practices what he preaches. He is a co-collaborator, mentor, and friend to his students. He has gone out of his way (literally *miles* out of his way) to show his support for our daughter.

"Mr. Solarz's unending kindness and validation gave our daughter the confidence she needed to excel this year. In short, he knows her 'love language,' and he spoke it well."

—*Liana Allison, Parent*

THE MARBLE THEORY MEETING

One Classroom Meeting I hold every year during the first week of school is called "Marble Theory." Marble Theory is something I use to help put intelligence into perspective for my students. Some students come into my classroom with very low self-esteem, due to low grades or poor performance in school. Others believe they are better than their peers because of past success in school. My goal with Marble Theory is to level the playing field. I want my students to realize that we are all equals with amazing gifts, talents, and interests. No one is better than anyone else. No one is worse. Once they understand we are all equals, increased respect leads to improved collaboration.

The Marble Theory states that we are all born with the same number of marbles in our brains. When we are born, these marbles are just in a big pile, but over time we allocate these marbles into cups. The cups represent our skills, talents, and abilities. We can have as many cups as we need and these cups are extremely specialized. For example, we don't have a cup for reading abilities. Instead, we have several cups for reading: one dedicated to decoding, one for literal comprehension, one for inferential comprehension, one for oral reading fluency, etc. But we also have cups dedicated to dribbling a basketball, drawing horses, telling jokes, and playing the flute.

In school, teachers usually spend time evaluating how many marbles students have in their academic cups, causing children to falsely assume that grades determine how intelligent they are. Kids who have many marbles in their cups dedicated to math, reading, writing, spelling, science, and social studies become known as the "smart kids." Children who have fewer marbles in those cups but more in their musical, athletic, interpersonal, or creative cups are not given the same accolades.

I contend that we are all equal in terms of intelligence and that intelligence needs to be measured differently. Because of grades and report cards, students learn to think of themselves as smart or dumb. Low grades do little more than disappoint and discourage students. High grades often create perfectionists and cause children to become extrinsically motivated. Although I am still required to give grades on report cards, I have taken away the focus on grades in our day-to-day activities. We embrace failure as a learning opportunity and as acknowledgment of taking risks. Instead of assigning grades on assignments, I give feedback that helps everyone grow. (You'll read more about feedback in the next chapter).

OUR DIFFERENCES HELP US GROW AND CHANGE AND EXPERIENCE NEW THINGS.

Understanding intelligence differently improves the way the kids in my classroom interact. Over the course of the year, my students stop disrespecting peers who are lower on the social ladder or who struggle academically and start asking *them* for help. If a student wants to teach a mini-lesson to the whole class, everyone joins them to learn what they are teaching, and everyone pays attention (for a period of time). The goal isn't simply to teach acceptance of differences, but to embrace each other's differences. What makes us different brings new perspectives and ways of thinking to the table. If we were all the same, we'd always do what we've always done. Our differences help us grow and change and experience new things. Once you get your students to see that, true collaboration will skyrocket.

USING SHARED READING TO TEACH EMPATHY

In addition to leveling the playing field and embracing our differences, students need to learn to empathize with each other. They need to know how to treat one another and know how to intervene appropriately when others are being mis-treated.

One of the ways that I teach empathy and work to build our classroom community (which in turn, improves collaboration) during the beginning of the school year is by reading *Wonder*, by R.J. Palacio. Here is an excerpt from the book's description on Amazon.com:

EMPATHY

> *"August Pullman was born with a facial difference that, up until now, has prevented him from going to a mainstream school. Starting fifth grade at Beecher Prep, he wants nothing more than to be treated as an ordinary kid—but his new classmates can't get past Auggie's extraordinary face."*

As we read *Wonder* together, our class bonds over Auggie's experiences. The book allows us to discuss sensitive topics such as bullying, including others in friendship groups, and overlooking students' special needs. What we read together helps convince each of my students that everyone should be treated with respect no matter what our differences.

I use a method similar to Read Aloud, called Shared Reading to teach *Wonder*. Just like Read Aloud, I read the story out loud to my students, sharing my thoughts, asking questions, and teaching reading strategies. But unlike Read Aloud, my students are actually required to read along with me. Over time, the Shared Reading experience improves students' reading fluency, as well as their spelling and vocabulary skills.

Because teaching empathy can be emotionally tough on children, I use a few strategies that help to de-personalize it at first. When I

SHARED READING ON A BUDGET

I don't have the budget to purchase twenty-seven copies of each novel that I choose to read with my class. And parents aren't always able to purchase those books either. Here's my solution: I purchase one Kindle version of the book. Using the free, Kindle for Mac app on my computer, I project the story onto our whiteboard. My students turn out the lights, grab pillows and their morning snacks, and I begin reading. It's a wonderful way to share a story together and improve our reading skills all at the same time.

introduce the idea of empathy, I purposely avoid personal feelings and focusing on us. Instead, we read a book that allows us to feel empathy for the character. In *Wonder*, the main character, Auggie, has craniofacial abnormalities and spends a lot of his childhood avoiding people and getting stared at. We spend a lot of time getting to know Auggie. When he is mistreated, we actually feel empathy for him. Books like this provide the perfect opportunity to teach how students should respond in difficult situations, or how to possibly prevent hurtful events in the first place. I always make a point to have students apply these strategies to their real lives. Because they've experienced empathy, they don't want others to feel what Auggie feels.

Shared Reading

Learning empathy often changes my students' perspectives toward some of their classmates. Although some of them may have been unkind in the past to certain individuals, they eventually understand that their behavior was hurtful and choose to stop it.

In the book, Auggie eventually makes a close friend, and he and Auggie are able to joke around about Auggie's shortcomings. When this boy playfully teases Auggie, my students are always offended and shocked, but Auggie is able to laugh at himself and doesn't mind the playful teasing because it's coming from someone he respects and knows respects him. We talk about this as a class, and we compare it to how best friends or siblings act together. Brothers and sisters can tease or call each other names, but no one else can do that to your sibling. You'd protect them from others! This is our initial attempt at learning how to empathize with each other.

One of my main goals each year is to create an environment where my students consider one another to be like siblings. Our comfort level together grows over time, and, although they eventually bicker like old married couples, they truly end up caring about each other. That's success in my book!

PROMOTING THE RIGHT KIND OF COMPETITION

I never understood how damaging competition could be until I focused on creating a collaborative classroom. Competition with others divides loyalty. It requires secrecy and focuses on doing better than others. Even collaborative competitions (team events) form cliques and perpetuate the idea of winning and losing (a final result) rather than learning (the process). Competition in the classroom may have a place, but it needs to be introduced carefully and used with a purpose! (See "Debates" in Chapter Seven.)

But there's a flip side to competition that can be very healthy and helpful. Although we don't focus our efforts on competition in our classroom, I assure you that each student continually competes to be *their* best. Internal competition is valuable. This kind of competition asks:

How can I do better next time?

Where can I make changes to this in order to make it better?

How can I help my peers do better?

Children need to learn the importance and value of personal drive but not at the *expense* of others in the classroom. So instead of focusing on winning, zero in on what it means to try one's hardest and how to bring peers along for the ride. (It brings new meaning to "No child left behind!")

Before I switched my focus to creating a collaborative environment, there were times when some students did things that made it look as though they didn't care about their learning, their classroom, or each other. Most of their actions were not devious or malicious, but I knew they were not helpful for their education. For example, my students have always practiced math skills together at a table or in partnerships. I used to assign a certain number of problems or pages and send them off to work. When grades and work completion were our main focus, I often noticed students dividing up the work and then giving each other the answers! When I announced that wasn't allowed, they gave me puzzled looks. Their faces would say, "Then why are you having us work together if we can't split up the work?" I realized that they were focused on task completion instead of mastering the skill.

When I shifted to teaching collaboration skills directly, I made sure to explain that, "The purpose of having you work together is that two heads are better than one. If you work on a problem together, you can share strategies and catch each other's mistakes. By the end of the year, you will have learned so much more than I taught you, because you worked together and helped each other."

CHILDREN NEED TO LEARN THE IMPORTANCE AND VALUE OF PERSONAL DRIVE BUT NOT AT THE EXPENSE OF OTHERS IN THE CLASSROOM.

Now, my students have a clear understanding of why they're working together. They don't try to split up the work because it's okay if they don't finish all of the problems. Incremental improvement is what we're about in our class, not work completion or even mastery. I work hard to make sure that their time spent practicing new skills is focused on understanding the skill and being able to transfer it to new situations. We no longer worry about getting through a large number of problems, which often resulted in a large number of errors and zero growth. The goal is quality, not quantity.

Throughout the day, students feel comfortable interrupting the class to ask for help, not from me, but from their peers via "Give Me Fives." They don't worry about not knowing everything and have grown to appreciate learning with and from those around them. Believe it or not, kids relish the chance to help each other. They drop what they're doing and take as much time as needed to show their peer how to do the task asked of them.

This sort of teamwork didn't happen in my classroom in the years before I shifted my focus to creating a collaborative community. Then, students felt afraid to ask for help because doing so was a sign of weakness; stopping to help a peer felt like a waste of time. The end result was a classroom in which individuals put themselves before the group. (I'm glad those days are over!)

I want to create a room full of learners, not perfectionists. I want my students to work hard because they choose to, not because they fear negative consequences. It's a paradigm shift for their young minds, but after a few months concentrating on incremental improvement, they realize that grades don't matter, learning does. They're not going to earn prizes or rewards. They're going to receive appreciation and feedback. (Taking the time to explain this philosophy at Parent Night during the first week of school equips parents to reinforce the focus on growth over mastery at home.)

A few years back, I had a great conversation with a parent of one of my students. Since we had a strong mutual respect for one another and had spoken on numerous occasions, she felt comfortable asking me a challenging question: "Do you think there would be any value to including more competition in the classroom?"

She explained herself while I gathered my thoughts. She said that she was in sales and had to compete each and every day against competitors, colleagues, time, etc. Competition was the main force that drove her day-to-day actions, and competition was what made her successful in her field.

I thought about it, and then asked her, "Do you agree that collaboration *and* competitiveness are both important skills that people might need to develop by the time they enter the work world?"

She said, "Yes."

"I do too," I said. "I wonder which skill students will practice more often in today's school system. I personally think they might be exposed to classrooms that focus on grades and put them into flexible groups based on abilities, or are chosen for teams based on strengths and skills, or are chosen for jobs based on being the best qualified for the job. They're going to learn how to compete along the way, but I wonder how often they'll get to focus intensely on interpersonal, collaborative skills without the possibility of negative consequences. I want them to be able to do that here in our classroom this year."

My parent whole-heartedly agreed and supported our classroom's collaborative nature. Although her career focused strongly on competition, she understood the value of collaboration in today's workplace. Ultimately, she was happy to see her child learning important interpersonal skills at a young age.

Kids learn how to compete through video games, sports, clubs, school, and everyday life! I want to make sure they learn how to work as a member of a team that looks out for, supports, and helps one another continue to grow and improve over time.

MYSTERY SKYPE: FRIENDLY COMPETITION THAT SPARKS COLLABORATION WORLDWIDE

Mystery Skypes provide a great opportunity for a collaborative experience that extends beyond your classroom's walls. A Mystery Skype is a forty-five- to sixty-minute critical-thinking challenge that your class takes part in while Skyping with another class somewhere else in the world. Your students' goal is to guess the other school's location (country, state, city, school name) before they guess yours. They do this while only asking yes and no questions of the other class.

Since students are assigned roles for this activity, collaboration becomes very important. In addition, the competitive spirit of the game really causes students to work together to maximize their abilities. You can, of course, use any video conferencing tool such as Google Hangouts or Face Time for this exercise.

During your first real Mystery Skype, students should be encouraged to review their responsibilities so know what to do and when they need to begin their job. Remind them that everyone is also a "Researcher" who is responsible for providing the "Questioners" with questions and answers. In keeping with the primary goal for a student-led classroom, the aim is to gradually release responsibility to your students. After a few Mystery Skypes, you will begin to see a class full of students working together to accomplish a very complex task, and they'll do so without your help.

STUDENT ROLES FOR MYSTERY SKYPE

Researchers—Look up answers to questions and help come up with questions to ask.

Greeters—Greet the partner school.

Sharers—Share something special about the school or area (but nothing that will give away our location).

Questioners—Ask the questions and keep the conversation going.

Questioners' Assistants—Quietly relay requests from questioners to the researchers and vice versa.

Photographers—Take photos while everyone is working and post them to Daily Photo Journal.

Videographers—Film the entire event and upload the video to YouTube.

Data Enterers—Enter questions and answers into the Mystery Skype spreadsheet (a Google form).

Closers—Wrap up the call and thank the other class.

Signers—Create and hold up signs that direct the other class for various reasons.

Task Masters—Walk around and *very nicely* help people stay on task.

Linkers—Add links to the Mystery Skype spreadsheet while researching.

Google Doc Cleaner-Uppers—Remove unnecessary tables, spaces, returns, etc. so the Mystery Skype doc stays neat and clean.

Question Focusers—Watch the Mystery Skype spreadsheet and help those who are asking questions that are not possible or too specific to ask better questions.

You can find more details about how we conduct Mystery Skypes in my classroom at LearnLikeaPirate.com.

MYSTERY SKYPE

Student Views on Peer Collaboration

"I think I collaborate pretty well with most of the class. I deal with conflict by either rock paper scissors or choose kind. I think it is important to work with others because you might not have the complete answer and your partner only has the other half, then you can put the two answers together and get the whole answer. Collaboration is important!" —*Bela*

"During math I helped my table when they did not understand how to do something in the math box. After that they understood how to do the problem. I should try to do more give me 5's. That would help being a leader." —*Lucas*

"During lit surcles my group was off task because we could not decide weather or not we would do a certain tipe of descushion I was the only one who wanted a certain descushon so i decided to go with mike's idea and then we figured the problem out faster because we decided as a group to vote." —*Demetri*

"During We the People, my group and I helped Demetri catch up on what we learned when he wasn't in the room. Our group worked together to come up with everything that we had learned in the reading." —*Kendall*

Peer
Collaboration

1. What is the purpose of giving students the power to interrupt the class when necessary?

2. Why is it important for teachers to make a conscious effort to provide opportunities for students to lead the class?

3. How do you encourage active leadership in your classroom? Passive leadership?

4. Do you use Classroom Meetings to discuss life skills or classroom concerns? Describe how you (would) do that?

5. Why is it important in a collaborative classroom to "level the playing field" so all students see one another as equals?

6. How do you teach your students empathy?

7. Why is it important to minimize competition in a collaborative classroom? How can you include competition carefully and meaningfully?

RESOURCES

---

[1] "CHARACTER COUNTS!" and "Six Pillars of Character" are registered trademarks of Josephson Institute, a 501(c)(3) nonprofit organization. Learn more at: http://charactercounts.org

[2] http://www.theleaderinme.org

IMPROVEMENT FOCUS VS. GRADE FOCUS

"Without continual growth and progress, such words as improvement, achievement, and success have no meaning."

—Benjamin Franklin

How often do you hear questions like these:

"How many points is this worth?"

"Can I earn extra credit?"

"Did you grade the tests yet?"

When students focus on grades rather than learning, extrinsic motivation drives their performance. In addition, their emotional well-being is often tied to those grades. Well-meaning parents then perpetuate the belief that grades matter above all else, because that was *their* school experience. Unfortunately, when grades, rewards, or punishments are a child's only motivation for doing well in school, he or she will find ways to work the system and miss the educational value of the lesson.

So how do you shift this decades-old paradigm for measuring accomplishment?

Start by downplaying grades and placing priority on personal improvement—shift the focus from external motivation to internal motivation. I touched a bit on the philosophy of incremental improvement in the previous chapter. Now we're going to look at several specific methods for helping students grasp the concept of constant improvement and integrate it into who they are and everything they do. Remember, education in your classroom isn't only about this year or even next year, it's about the people your students will grow into. It's about instilling in them a love for learning. Focusing on formative assessment that takes a student from their Personal Point A to their Personal Point B will be more valuable than any number in a gradebook.

That being said, you can't get around grades in schools today. Report cards are part of the system. My students receive report cards three times per year, but we only talk about them to reduce their importance. I explain that report cards are intended to report our progress to parents and other teachers. The data contained in these documents can be used to make informed decisions further down the line, but they aren't something to worry about or fear.

My belief is that grades shouldn't earn rewards or privileges, nor should they earn negative consequences or punishments. Likewise, points, badges, and rewards can *feel* great—when you're earning them. Winning feels wonderful. But not all students earn enough points or badges or rewards to feel like they've won. Some students struggle every day just to stay afloat. In a classroom filled with extrinsic motivators, these students get worn down. Despite all of their hard work, they never do better than even half the class. Sure, sometimes a teacher gives them a "Hardest Worker" certificate or a badge for "Perseverance." But deep down, students know their effort rarely equates to what some other students receive without even trying. So, they eventually stop trying. Grades shouldn't earn rewards or privileges, nor should they earn negative consequences or punishments.

GRADES SHOULDN'T EARN REWARDS OR PRIVILEGES, NOR SHOULD THEY EARN NEGATIVE CONSEQUENCES OR PUNISHMENTS.

In contrast, students who receive high marks despite low effort learn that school is easy. In their minds, focusing on improvement is unnecessary. Why revise your work when you already have an "A"? These students regress with regard to learning because they know their reward has already been earned; they no longer have to work for it.

I don't want to create that kind of environment in my classroom. I want all of my students to know they matter and that their place in our classroom is just as important as anyone else's. Every child needs to be encouraged to continue learning and improving. Assessment and feedback, rather than a focus on grades, pushes students toward constant growth.

I want my students to work hard because they understand the value of the work, and it's my job to help them understand that value. I want their reward to be their enjoyment of the learning process. I *don't* want them worrying about what grade they'll receive when the work is done! For that matter, I don't want them to think learning is ever "done." Rather than "finishing" a project, why not continue to give feedback and expect improvements to be made? Why are we so focused on finality that we have to assign a summative grade to everything?

Big Ideas, Common Core Standards, and twenty-first century skills drive assessment in our classroom rather than content standards. Because of this, my students don't take many tests or quizzes. Students don't receive grades on any of their work or projects either. They do, however, receive regular feedback. Skills and comprehension can be better assessed through observations while students are working. Therefore, we take the time we used to spend studying, taking tests, and going over those tests, and devote it to working and learning more!

IMPROVING THROUGH EFFECTIVE FEEDBACK

Most school days, I spend the bulk of my time walking around the room talking with students. The atmosphere is generally casual and students are never concerned when I approach them. I observe what they're doing, ask questions, and share my thoughts. My feedback guides their thinking in the moment, as well as in future situations in our classroom.

No grades are associated with this time. I don't walk around with my laptop or a clipboard doling out grades based on what I see. My feedback comes with no strings attached. I've earned my students' respect by demonstrating that I genuinely care about them *and* their progress, so they listen when I share insights and offer instruction.

Teacher feedback is necessary for our students' success. As teachers, we can be most effective by remembering that every child is at a different point for different tasks, and that some tasks are more significant than others. Feedback, then, should focus on what's most important for each child. The best way to provide truly effective, personalized feedback is to constantly observe each student's actions. That's why I walk around the room, watch my students at work, and respond to what I see.

Feedback can be offered in countless ways. Sometimes, I leave comments in their Google Docs. Sometimes, I whisper advice while they're writing. Sometimes, I pull a group aside to talk with them about my observations. Sometimes, I sit with a team and work through a problem with them.

Recently, I noticed one of my students getting frustrated with the members of her group. She raised her voice and started barking out commands. In an attempt to lead the group, her emotions took over. I spoke to her privately and asked her if her behavior displayed good leadership skills or had crossed over into bossiness. She admitted she was getting bossy and said she would try to calm down and lead with kindness. I didn't try to make her feel badly, but I encouraged her to be aware of her tone and work to improve it. The immediate feedback empowered her to make the change and feel positive about it. Since there was no grade or tangible consequence associated with the experience, she felt no remorse or guilt. This small mistake provided an opportunity to grow and improve. I also let her know I was proud of her for taking the risk of trying to lead her group.

Sometimes feedback on one student's or team's work can benefit everyone. In those cases, I share it immediately with the whole class. Constant observation also makes it possible for me to anticipate many potential problems before they happen. When I see a complication on the horizon, I have a choice of either offering a helpful hint to keep them moving forward or staying quiet and letting them resolve the issue on their own. If I perceive an opportunity for a valuable learning experience (one that would be ruined if I warned them), I keep quiet.

For many students, constant feedback can be tough to accept at first. They're not used to being so frequently corrected or praised by their teacher. It might feel like nit-picking to some, but once we talk about why I do it, they understand. As I work to build a relationship with each student, they come to appreciate the constructive feedback even more.

Speaking to students in present or future tense helps them accept feedback as constructive. For example:

Rather than saying: "You shouldn't have done it this way; you should've done it this way."

Say this: "Next time, I'd like you to do it this way because…" Or, "Can you try this way instead?" Or, "Are you displaying good leadership skills right now, or could you do better?"

Speaking in the past tense makes students feel as if there's no way to fix their mistake or failure. (What's done is done.) In contrast, speaking in the present or future tense demonstrates that learning is a process. Even if their attempt wasn't perfect, they're making progress toward what's expected. Affirm that they will have more chances to do it better—and you have confidence in their ability to succeed! Otherwise you wouldn't offer feedback. Make sure students understand that failure is a natural part of the learning process; it is a stepping stone to success. When you create a classroom culture where failure is embraced and has no grade associated with it, students will embrace your feedback because they *want* to improve.

IMPROVING CLASSROOM BEHAVIOR

We've all read about how to handle discipline problems in our classrooms. We know all about attention-seeking behaviors and power struggles. But what if I told you nearly all discipline problems go away when students constantly have the attention of their peers and you've given them so much power that they have nothing left to fight for? Done correctly, empowering students to run the classroom and direct their learning eliminates most discipline problems. (Be sure to combine that empowerment with genuine caring. We must take time to build those relationships!)

SET THE EXPECTATION

In our classroom, we have one rule: "Be a good person." I've used the Six Pillars of Character® outlined by the Josephson Institute Center for Youth Ethics[1] and *The Seven Habits of Highly Effective People*[2] described by Stephen R. Covey. Everyone in the classroom, including me, is expected to follow these pillars and habits! They are:

CHARACTER COUNTS!®

1. Respect
2. Responsibility
3. Trustworthiness
4. Fairness
5. Caring
6. Citizenship

CHARACTER COUNTS!

SEVEN HABITS OF HIGHLY EFFECTIVE PEOPLE®

1. Be Proactive
2. Begin with the End in Mind
3. Put First Things First
4. Think Win-Win
5. Seek First to Understand, Then to Be Understood
6. Synergize
7. Sharpen the Saw

IDENTIFY THE CONSEQUENCES

In my class, students are generally well-behaved, and discipline is rarely an issue. To maintain consistency, I use a behavior management system that includes:

1. A warning
2. A behavior point
3. A Work-It-Out

Students receive warnings more as feedback to discourage certain behaviors. A warning is not perceived as a big deal. I give them often at the beginning of the year to support the rules of the classroom. I have even been known to give myself warnings when I've accidentally broken the classroom rules! A warning is a gentle reminder to each of us about the importance of following the six pillars of character.

A behavior point is a second warning for a similar misbehavior during the same day. Originally, I kept track of behavior points in order to have conversations with students if they weren't making progress toward improving their behavior. I've since discovered that, in our student-led classroom that focuses on improvement and welcomes failure, students will tell me if they already have been given their warning for a given day and will ask for a behavior point instead! They know there's nothing to be fearful of, but that they need to try to make improvements.

A Work-It-Out is the third level of our behavior-management system. Students are asked to go into the hallway and fill out a "think sheet" regarding their behavior. Students receive a Work-It-Out for a third strike on a given day or for a more serious offense, where a warning doesn't seem appropriate. After the student completes the form, we have a one-on-one discussion about what happened to clear the air and to help prevent repeated mistakes. During this discussion, my goal is to make sure they care enough, but not so much that they cry. No mistake in class should cause tears.

When you constantly provide feedback and stay aware of escalating situations, most problems can be prevented or caught early on so that they don't require a consequence. One important thing I have learned through the years is that giving a student a warning is far better than getting frustrated. I use warnings and behavior points as ways to correct my students' behavior rather than raising my voice or giving the entire class a consequence. Students have come to under-stand that warnings, behavior points, and Work-it-Outs are a form of corrective feedback and rarely get worked up about them. But they also understand the importance of learning from their mistakes and trying their hardest to avoid repeating them.

IMPROVING RESULTS AND RETENTION

Rigor is different for each student. What is hard for one is easy for another, so I don't plan "rigorous lessons." Instead, I provide oppor-tunities for students to find the rigor in our everyday work. Con-stant improvement, rather than mastery, is our focus. I've found ePortfolios to be an ideal tool for helping students improve their work and increase their retention.

ePortfolios

Prior to using ePortfolios in the class-room, I was notorious for teaching a lesson, having the students complete an activity, and quickly moving on to the next lesson, without taking much time to allow my students to think about what they just learned. An inch deep and a mile wide was my motto! Unfortunately, this kind of one-time instruction doesn't translate into permanent learning. Students often can't remember what they did yesterday if they don't have time to reflect and process! ePort-folios force me to slow down, give the students an opportunity to explain to me, in writing or through video, what they've learned, and to create an emotional attachment by explaining what was easy or difficult, fun or boring, familiar or foreign to them. They require each student to contemplate and internalize what they've learned.

Just like traditional paper portfolios, ePortfolios provide a space to collect and organize students' work throughout the school year. This collection allows them to see (and take pride in) their growth and to reflect on their efforts. The difference is that the blog format of an ePortfolio offers the added benefits of the ability to share the students' work with a global audience and to make ongoing improvements or additions.

An ePortfolio blog post's format and content will vary from task to task and subject to subject as the objective of the lesson changes. The typical format includes:

- A title that describes the Big Idea or concept.

- A picture or video of the process or final product from the activity.

- Answers to reflection and synthesis questions that guide each child to successfully demonstrate their understanding of the concept.

In our class, students create more ePortfolio entries in science and social studies than they do in any other subject. Students take pictures and record videos during experiments, labs, and observations in science. They type in their predictions, display their data, and reflect on their results all within the same blog post. They even learn how to use web tools to make and embed graphs and data charts into their blogs.

We no longer use paper in science or social studies because all directions are posted online and all work is "turned in" via ePortfolio entries. No more lost papers. No more "My dog ate my homework" or "I

BLENDED LEARNING

left it at home," excuses. Everything is done online and published immediately.

Because our ePortfolios are on blogs that are open to the world, they provide my students with a more authentic, global audience to explain their process and show their products. Students also have the opportunity to look at a respected peer's work and even model their peers' posts in the future. I call this "silent collaboration" (a 180-degree turn from the days of calling it cheating). I want my students to learn together, model and follow positive behavior, and benefit from one another's mistakes and successes. Not all collaboration has to be done verbally or include back-and-forth dialogue!

EACH STUDENT'S EPORTFOLIO PROVIDES ME WITH AN EXCELLENT CACHE OF EVIDENCE THAT SHOWS GROWTH OVER TIME.

I have been using reflective ePortfolios in my classroom for several years now, and have found them to be more effective than worksheets or quizzes for getting children to synthesize the information they've learned. Each student's ePortfolio provides me with an excellent cache of evidence that shows growth over time. And since I believe no assignment is ever finished for good, students are encouraged (sometimes strongly) to revise old ePortfolio entries, based on new instruction or skills they've mastered. Bonus: There's no need to provide worksheets to practice basic skills, like capitalization and end punctuation, when students can go back and correct their own work!

Getting students to reflect on their learning and express their thoughts in writing can be a challenge. I have found two ways that have seemed to improve the written reflections at the end of ePortfolio entries.

TELL ME MORE

Although this first option may seem simple, the results are significant. I provide students with specific questions to guide their reflections. They must answer each question with at least two sentences. The first sentence should answer the question the best way possible. The second sentence should "Tell me more."

It's easy for students to answer questions with a single word or a sentence. But when you ask them to "tell me more," they are forced to deeply consider the lesson. This is where you really see what they're thinking! Their reflections will provide you with more evidence of their understanding of the activity than any worksheet, quiz, or test could! This addition doesn't require a large investment of additional time, yet it gets students to elaborate more on their learning experience.

Questions for reflection can and should vary. You could ask students to interpret their data and extrapolate trends, apply what they've learned to new situations, or predict how new information or discoveries could have affected events in history. Use your imagination and stretch their thinking! Keep in mind that the questions should ask students to reflect and synthesize, not remember and regurgitate. Here's an example of questions I asked my students after completing a unit on energy:

1. What was your favorite station? Why?

2. Which object was most difficult to figure out? Why was it so hard to figure out the energy transfers in this object?

3. Which three stations do you feel very confident that you figured out correctly? Describe one and explain what made it so obvious.

4. Was it always possible to know for sure what kinds of energy transfers occurred?

5. Go to our classroom YouTube channel and spend a little time watching other students' videos of stations that you think you and your partner(s) might have gotten wrong. Try to find a group or two that explained a particular station better than you did. Which group do you want to give a shout out to for doing a good job explaining a particular station? List their names, the station they explained, and the URL to their video so I can watch it!

HERE'S ONE STUDENT'S UNEDITED RESPONSE:

1. *My favorite station were the pop up frogs because i liked watching them pop up really high in the air. It showed me a lot how elastic energy works.*

2. *The plasma ball was the hardest station because it was to come up with anything it would be except for electrical energy. We made the video at the next station it was so hard.*

3. *I think the pop up frogs , love thermometer, anddominos were the easiest. The pop up frogs Were really easy because they moved, went back down , and were elastic hint hint.*

4. *Yes it was very possible because at every station because we could at least figure out one transfer at every station. But the others were really difficult.*

5. *I will give a shout out to Nicole and Payton for the gailieo thermometer and not just because it was on the website. They helped me understand it better because me and Demetri didn't understand it at first.*

From this student's answers, I can see what he enjoyed and understood, as well as what areas weren't as easy to grasp. And, as I mentioned earlier, a post like this that was written early in the school year can be revisited to add new information or insights and to correct punctuation, capitalization, and spacing.

THINKING DEEPER

Although most ePortfolio entries end with specific reflection and synthesis questions, I sometimes prefer for students to reflect on the learning experience without my direct guidance. Therefore, I have developed a generic reflection process to bc used when questions aren't provided. This process works well but requires a little more time.

Step 1: Describe what happened or what you did during the lesson.

Step 2: Interpret how things went by using one (or more) of these sets of terms:
- Strengths and Weaknesses
- Successes and Setbacks

Step 3: What have you learned due to this experience?

Step 4: Answer one (or more) of these questions:
- What can you do to improve your learning?
- How will you extend your learning past what is expected?

I usually introduce this method midway through the school year, after students have become comfortable with the reflective process. My goal is to have students consider these questions holistically and write their thoughts in a paragraph or two (rather than in isolation, which is their tendency early in the year). Ultimately, it doesn't matter when you introduce this process. The key is giving appropriate feedback so students are able to revise and improve their work. With a little coaching, they will be able to write reflections that get deep into their thinking and provide you (and their other readers) with a strong understanding of what they've learned.

ePortfolios and reflective questions challenge students to take their learning to another level. I've noticed in my own classroom that, when students spend ample time thinking about what they've learned, they retain the information. And that's a win! After all, I'm not just asking my students to learn concepts temporarily or remember things for a test. I'm asking them to internalize information and skills so they can use them for the rest of their lives.

IMPROVING INDEPENDENT THINKING AND COLLABORATION WITH *HOMEWORK CLUB*

Maintaining ePortfolios can help students in many ways, but it can also be very challenging. Since students require different amounts of time to complete tasks, some don't finish their ePortfolio entries before the period ends—which means homework. Unfortunately, not everyone has access to computers or tablets at home. And some students won't have a strong enough understanding of how to edit blog posts without assistance. A solution that meets the needs of all of my students is *Homework Club.*

Every day, my students have the opportunity to come to school early, stay in during lunch or recess, or stay after school for thirty minutes. (Since I sometimes have meetings, days off, and other conflicts, I post a schedule in class each week to let students know when Homework Club is open.) During this time, students can get assistance with their work or just complete assignments on their own. They also have access to our classroom's technology. Siblings and friends are invited. After school, students from the middle school and high school often visit to say, "Hi." Teachers come in to collaborate. Parents stop by to ask questions or gather their child's forgotten materials. (We have to work on that!) It is often quite a rockin' place! Of course, it can also be distracting at times. Even so, I love Homework Club!

Students work independently, collaboratively, or with me during Homework Club. Frequently, students use this time to get more face-to-face time with their peers while working on a collaborative assignment. As I was writing this section of the book on my lunch break, eleven students came into "Lunch Recess Homework Club" to make props for their Readers' Theater presentations the following day. These independent and collaborative experiences help students develop executive functioning skills, reinforce student-led learning during the school day, and remind students that they can accomplish great things when they work together.

Independent thinking doesn't only happen in the classroom; it continues at home when they ask their parents to take them to school early so they can get help with a homework problem or finish a blog entry on our classroom computers. I love finding out my students have arranged to meet at Homework Club to complete an assignment or to study for a test. These are important skills that many are practicing for the first time in their lives.

CRITICAL PEER FEEDBACK— QUALITY BOOSTERS

In the past, when I asked my students to peer-revise a writing piece or give suggestions for improvement after a presentation, I was hard-pressed to find much value in most comments. Most students were either too worried about how critical feedback would make their peer feel, or they didn't know how to properly identify or evaluate skills. Written suggestions made some students feel inferior to the person who revised their paper. Face-to-face suggestions felt awkward because students could see their peers' reactions—and few people enjoy hearing about their mistakes!

I BELIEVED MY STUDENTS' ABILITIES COULD GROW EXPONENTIALLY IF I COULD INCREASE THE AMOUNT OF CRITICAL FEEDBACK THEY RECEIVED.

Last year, I was reading over my students' Passion Time project reflections and watching their videos when I had a realization: Each of my twenty-seven students were relying on *my* feedback in order to improve their projects from one round to the next. (See page 215 for more information about Passion Time projects.) They frequently received compliments from their peers and from students and teachers online. But they rarely received constructive feedback that could help them improve their future projects. All criticism came from me.

That realization felt intense and intimidating. I knew how long it took me to get through every project each round. I also knew that some students needed to improve multiple aspects of their projects. If I pointed out every deficiency, my criticism, no matter how constructive or positively phrased, might feel overwhelming.

I believed my students' abilities could grow exponentially if I could increase the amount of critical feedback they received, so I decided to revisit the idea of peer feedback. I understood that, first, students needed to know how to give critical peer feedback in a way that was constructive and honest but still kind and esteem-building. Second, but equally important, they had to learn to accept critical feedback as an attempt to help them improve, rather than an attack on their abilities, a lesson that fit in nicely with our philosophy of revision and improvement over time vs. perfectionism and grades. The lesson was called "Quality Boosters." Here's how I explained it to the class:

> In our class, we don't care much about grades. We don't care much about who's better than whom. We care about working together to become the strongest "Me" we can each become. We welcome people's opinions about our work, because, when they take the time to give us their opinion (even when it's negative), they are helping us improve in some way. And our goal is constant improvement! We don't care where we start from—we care where we finish. We don't care who is performing better than us. We care that we are performing to our highest level possible!

Today, we are going to watch one another's Passion Project videos and read their KWHLAQ Charts and Reflections. We are going to do so with a critical eye—one that looks for things that could be improved. We aren't going to act judgmental or act like we know everything and others know nothing. We won't put anyone down or make anyone feel stupid. We are going to identify areas where our peers can improve to help them be the best that they can be. We will call our critical feedback "Quality Boosters" because our goal will be to boost the quality of one another's Passion Projects!

We won't feel awkward or rude because we're helping them improve their craft. We're helping them make a better product. We're helping them feel more proud of themselves tomorrow than they feel today. When they read our critical feedback, they will know we are giving them these suggestions because we feel it will make their projects even better than they are today. They know this is an assignment and not someone putting them down. They know what your goal is, because it's the same goal they have themselves: to help one another improve our projects!

Let's brainstorm some ways that we can make critical feedback more bearable. Should we be blunt and vague and just tell them that their video stinks? Or is it better to be polite and specific about ways they can make their video better? Should we say that their written reflection is short and that they should have tried harder? Or should we explain that a longer written reflection would have clarified what they learned during this round of Passion Time? Polite, specific feedback will help our peers improve their craft. Blunt, generic feedback will only hurt their feelings and cause them to be defensive or dismissive.

I have three ways that you can write a Quality Booster so that your peer will handle your critical feedback positively:

1. Start by saying you have a Quality Booster for them! They'll know right away that you are going to offer a suggestion that may be critical of their work. They'll be prepared and will probably handle it better!

2. Start or end with a specific compliment! When some-one feels that you honestly appreciate their work, they are more likely to accept your critical feedback. (Some people suggest having a compliment before and after the Quality Booster. That's called a Compliment Sand-wich!)

3. Write your suggestion as a question rather than a statement. Instead of telling your peer what to change, ask them if it might sound better if... or you wonder if people would understand it better if... You don't seem superior to them if you're just wondering something!

After a short discussion in which my students offered their sug-gestions for writing quality comments, I assigned them each one person (by randomly pulling Popsicle sticks) to give feedback. When they had done a *great* job on that one, they could go on to any other projects that they were excited to review. After about twenty minutes, I asked everyone to read the comments that they had received and reply back thoughtfully. The responses (and the critical comments) turned out to be excellent! We are now using this routine at the end of every round of Passion Time and every major writing piece.

Here are a few of my students' thoughts on Quality Boosters and on feedback in general:

"I love to comment on other people's blogs because I like to see what smart and unique projects they came up with.

I also like to see the kids' videos are. The blogs benefit me in two ways. I like when people give me compliments, because it makes me feel good, important, and like I did a good job. But, I also like the criticism because it makes me realize what I need to improve on for further rounds." —Emma

"I liked commenting on other's work because I feel I am noting ways that they can judge themselves if they can't do it themselves. I also liked reading comments I received because they showed fresh points of view to help me. They help me get stronger by allowing me to notice the flaws of others, and saying, 'Does that apply to me?'" —Julia

"Because then it gives us a idea of what to do on our next passion time. Because then you can see what other people think would make it better because you always want to be improving on everything you can." —Sam K.

"I liked how we could compliment on other people because it made them feel better and could get feedback on what they could change. The comments were a benefit to me because I could figure out what I did very well, what could've been changed, and what I forgot if anything. But it also it is helpful to get feedback on what you just did and see what other people thought about your project." —Justin

"I like to have access to give my peers feedback and the same to me. I think it is important to give feedback because you can give ideas that can make people do better on their projects." —Jack

"I liked commenting on other people's blogs because we could let them know what we liked about their blog, and what they could do to make it even better. The comments can benifit us because then we can see things that we could do better on our blog because other people pointed them out, and we might not have seen them if other people haden't have pointed them out." —Abby

"I liked commenting on the other peoples projects because I could get to see what other people were doing and what other cool stuff was going on in the classroom. It gets you to think about what was good, and what could be improved, and also it helps you see what you could improve on. Comments help you because you get to know what other people think about it, and also ways that you could improve and get better in future rounds." —Connor

"I liked to be able to comment on others blogs and passion time projects because, it allowed me to help perfect others mistakes for the next round and the long run. I liked it when others commented on my passion time project for two reasons. One reason is it makes me feel like people care about my project. The other is that I can correct myself in ways I can't see by myself. These comments benefit me in a very good way and make me better than I already am. As Mr. Solarz calls them, Quality Boosters, do these amazing things." —Michael

When you remind your students of the importance of critical feedback and give them enough time to be successful, they end up making you proud!

STUDENT VIEWS ON IMPROVEMENT FOCUS VS. GRADE FOCUS

"I was doing my homework for WTP and I answered a question, but I felt as though I could have answered it better, so I went and revised it, and added to it." —*Isabela*

"When Mr. Solarz gives me feedback in math I really love the feedback because when he explains to me what I did wrong I like that he does it because next time I know not to make the wrong mistake I like Mr. Solarz' feedback that he gives everybody." —*Emily*

"When I made the first draft for my 100 word story today. I thought it needed a little more thought for it. I kept thinking it needs another character but who? Then Alison asked if we could use each other in our story's. So that solved my problem. So once I had a good juicy story and another character. I thought I had a great story base." —*Payton*

"I think it is good that grades don't matter and that the only thing matters is improvement. If we are improving that means that were good students learning new things." —*Madi*

IMPROVEMENT FOCUS VS. GRADE FOCUS

1. How often do you give specific feedback to your students?

2. During which activities can you begin to offer regular feedback to your students?

3. How can you teach your students to be more focused on improvement and revision, rather than completion and grades?

4. How can you increase your students' intrinsic motivation so they don't rely on grades for extrinsic motivation?

5. How can you change the mindset of students who believe grades are their reward for hard work?

6. How can you encourage your students to keep improving their assignments, even after a unit has been completed?

7. How can you enlist the services of your students to provide meaningful, constructive feedback?

RESPONSIBILITY

"Students must have initiative; they should not be mere imitators. They must learn to think and act for themselves—and be free."

—Cesar Chavez

It's the end of a long week. I've just high-fived all of my students and wished them a happy weekend. I unwind and walk around the room with the intent of straightening up our workspace so it's ready for the next week. But as I look around, it's obvious just how much my students do without having to be asked or reminded by me. Our classroom calendar has been updated to the new month, and the days are even in the correct spots! The whiteboard has been erased and cleaned with a solution that makes it look brand new. Every chair in the room, including those at the center group of hexagonal tables, has been neatly stacked. All of the student mail has been distributed and taken home by each child. The pencil sharpeners are devoid of shavings and the computers are all shut down. I'm so thankful to be able to just grab my belongings and head out to enjoy my weekend!

Throughout our entire day, students take responsibility for seeing to our classroom's needs, and they do so without much fanfare or interference by me. They do what needs to be done—without seeking attention for their efforts! Students think for themselves and of one another. They maximize their time-on-task and anticipate what comes next in class. My students' sense of ownership not only makes our class operate more smoothly, the skills and character they are developing will serve them well as they progress through their school years and beyond.

Of course, to get these kinds of results, students must be entrusted with responsibilities. They need to know it takes everyone's help and participation to successfully run the classroom. Students need to feel needed and relied upon. And they need to know what tasks need to get done each day and week, as well as *how* to do them. When you set the expectation of student leadership and then provide space and encouragement for them to take control, I know you'll be impressed at their abilities. You'll also discover that the more responsibility students are given, the more likely they are to find success. Over time, personal accountability becomes a part of their thinking process.

CLASSROOM RESPONSIBILITY— PUTTING STUDENTS IN CHARGE

At the beginning of each year, we hold a classroom meeting during which I explain my philosophy that students have equal power as the teacher in the operation of the classroom. I let them know they can do anything I can do (within reason) and they don't have to be asked or ask permission to step up to the task. My expectation is that they identify what needs to be done, figure out the best way to do it, and then make it happen. I assure them I will provide feedback if they've done anything wrong, and I promise not to get upset at their mistakes. I want them to know from the onset that I will be proud of them for taking risks. This discussion empowers students to take initiative and do what they think needs to be done to make our classroom run smoothly!

Once the stage is set for students to take charge of the classroom, it's time to provide them with opportunities to lead! In our classroom, as with yours, several tasks need to be done every day. Some of these tasks are fairly boring and wouldn't get done if they weren't assigned to someone, while other tasks are highly sought after. I assign these "classroom jobs" to individuals. In addition, hundreds of other responsibilities need to be done but aren't specified or assigned to individuals. Instead, these are considered "collaborative responsibilities" and can and should be done by anyone (and everyone).

CLASSROOM JOBS

Every year, depending on the number of students I have, I create a list of important classroom jobs. Now, there are probably hundreds of tasks you can hand over to students, but most are collaborative responsibilities (explained further in the next section). The jobs I assign to students are those that must get done every day for the classroom to function properly.

Over the years, I have learned something important about assigning jobs to individuals versus sharing responsibilities among the whole class. Creating jobs and assigning tasks to students ensures important jobs get done. Just be sure to keep many (or even most) responsibilities free for everyone to share. If you create jobs for every task, you rob students of countless opportunities to take charge! Assigned jobs can become a really bad thing in a student-led classroom if not done correctly. They can:

- Put all the responsibility for a task on one person, meaning that everyone else will avoid the task, even if they see it needs to be done,

- Make students feel as though responsibilities will be assigned by the teacher, rather than allowing students to have the authority to complete tasks on their own,

- Force students to think individually, rather than collectively,

- Place blame on individuals when jobs aren't done, causing unnecessary conflict.

That being said, I assign a few carefully determined jobs as a means of introducing the concept of citizenship in our classroom. We all have jobs to do, as well as dozens of other responsibilities. (Everything that isn't a formal "job" becomes a collaborative responsibility.) In addition, whenever we notice that a student's individual job hasn't been done, we either remind them to do it or do it for them and let them know. That way, we all share responsibility for the operation of the class, rather than rely on and blame others when things aren't done. If we all work hard to help our classroom operate efficiently and effectively, then we will work in a happier, friendlier environment.

IF YOU CREATE JOBS FOR EVERY TASK, YOU ROB STUDENTS OF COUNTLESS OPPORTUNITIES TO TAKE CHARGE!

Classroom jobs usually require some specialized skills, which are passed on from student to student as jobs change. The following is a partial list of the jobs in my classroom this year. You can change or add to this list based on your classroom's specific needs.

Attendance Takers record who is absent and what lunch everyone is ordering. The count is due to the office within fifteen minutes of our day starting. If I took five minutes to do this every morning, I would be wasting valuable instruction time! Two students are assigned to hunt down their classmates and make sure everyone has moved their magnets before starting their day!

Mail Distributors pass out all of the flyers and packets that get sent home via "backpack mail" every week. Without Mail Distributors, I would be getting phone calls from parents who are upset about missing important notices!

The **Absent-Minded Professors** are responsible for taking care of students who are absent. They fill out a form letting them know everything we did during the day, gather supplies and materials for them to complete their work at home, and bring down their materials to the office to be picked up by their parents.

The **Magnet Mover** moves back all of the magnets each day on our Attendance/Lunch Count board. If they don't get moved back before the next day, we don't know who is absent.

The **Lunch Bin Transporters** bring the lunch bin down to the cafeteria so students don't have to bring their lunch bags out to recess. They also bring it back to the classroom on their way in from recess.

The **Laptop Cart Monitor** checks the Laptop Schedule every day, gets the laptop cart when we have it checked out, and brings it back when we are done (and plugs it in). He or she also makes sure all of the computers are plugged in correctly.

The **Pencil Sharpener Dumper** (A great name, I know!) is responsible for emptying the electronic pencil sharpeners before they overflow with shavings. Prior to assigning this important job, we were breaking too many of our sharpeners!

The **Morning Greeter** says "Good Morning" to everyone who walks in and reminds students of the daily goal and to move their magnets.

The **Afternoon Reminderer** asks students as they leave the classroom for the day if they have stacked their chairs, picked up their mail, and completed their jobs.

The **Recapper** is responsible for conducting our end-of-the-day classroom discussion about homework and finishing our classwork. (See REARJMCL on page 136.) The day's recap is written on the board and posted online, as well as copied by every student in their own Assignment Notebooks.

The **Evaluator** is responsible for leading our end-of-the-day discussion looking at how we did and how we can improve. He or she also determines if we earned any free time or points towards a new privilege or gift.

The **Announcer** is responsible for leading our end-of-the-day discussion about upcoming events, giving important reminders, and telling the students to get their mail, stack their chairs, do their jobs if they haven't already, reset the room, and line up.

So many things need to get done in a classroom each day. It would be impossible to identify all of the tasks and fairly distribute them to students as formal "jobs." Encourage active thinking and decision making to foster a sense of ownership and collaborative responsibility in your classroom.

COLLABORATIVE RESPONSIBILITY— WORKING TOGETHER FOR A BETTER LEARNING EXPERIENCE

Early in my teaching career, I struggled with the idea of assigning individuals specific roles in small group projects. While a division of work seemed appropriate, I wondered if assigned roles kept students from jumping in and using their natural talents and skills. At the same time, I worried that pre-defined roles might force individuals to do certain tasks that weren't a good fit for their unique skill sets. After spending some time studying the concept of transfer from Grant Wiggins and Jay McTighe[1], I also began to wonder how my students would translate skills to other situations if they practiced them only when they were assigned a role.

TRANSFER

Those concerns led me to change to the way I instruct students while they're working in groups. These days, I teach all of my students all of the tasks that need to get done for their group and ask them to share the responsibility. Yes, some students dominate and some sit back and let others lead. Over time, however, the workload evens out, due to the feedback students receive from their peers and me. The process of discovering and defining their own roles empowers them to transfer their learning to new situations in the future.

I apply that same approach to the needs of our classroom. When it comes to whole-class, procedural tasks such as transitioning between subjects, pushing in their chairs, or re-shelving the books in our classroom library, I could easily create jobs (roles) for students to do these daily tasks. But what message would that send? I'd be saying that students don't have to keep the class on schedule, or push in chairs when they see them in the way, or re-shelve their own books— because someone else would always do those jobs for them. That message creates an environment similar to a home in which parents constantly clean up after their children and never expect them to clean up after themselves. I want all of my students to be responsible for *everything* within their power. Therefore, rather than assigning roles for everything that needs to be done, I limit classroom jobs to those who help monitor the progress of the class.

Collaborative responsibility means *all* students are expected to notice and complete certain tasks, rather than relying on specific individuals to do them. I want all of my students to develop the ability to identify problems and determine possible solutions. The goal is for students to actively take care of our classroom, rather than wait for others to do so. When they're encouraged to be constantly aware of what needs to be done, they don't expect others to tell them what to do and when to do it. Instead, they learn to be leaders and show initiative and drive—skills that aren't often focused on in school today.

OPPORTUNITIES FOR COLLABORATIVE RESPONSIBILITY

If we want our students to be collectively responsible for a large number of tasks in our classrooms, then we as the teachers need to identify those tasks and give students the opportunity to complete them. Student leadership doesn't happen by chance! The first time my students miss an opportunity to complete a collaborative responsibility, I do it for them. Immediately afterward, I do a "Give Me Five" and tell them I expect them to take responsibility for that task in the future. The second time they miss the opportunity to complete the same task, I quietly ask a student to complete the task and do a "Give Me Five" announcing that it's someone else's turn next time. If students continue to neglect their responsibilities, I will either choose to make it a permanent job or apply a natural consequence that will motivate them to try harder next time.

For example, when my students forget to lead our transition from one subject to another, it may cause us to be late to lunch or recess. That's a natural consequence that wouldn't happen if they led the class to start transitioning earlier. Or when my students have indoor recess and don't start cleaning up on their own, it sometimes can cut into our next lesson. I tell them about the importance of being on time and following our schedule and then say that those minutes will come out of the next fun lesson. Experiencing the natural consequence helps my students understand how their leadership directly affects their happiness. The better leaders they become, the happier they become.

Our daily schedule is posted on a small monitor in class, and transition times are listed with each activity. Students learn they must allow the right amount of time between activities. For example, to go from reading to lunch is a quick transition, but we have to move some tables back to where they belong, so we allow two to three minutes for transitioning. Going from Social Studies to Math requires that computers are put away, new materials are gathered, and several students switch classes. This transition takes about five minutes. Transitioning from one activity to the next requires that they identify the necessary steps and mentally calculate the time it takes to do all those steps. I love the thinking skills that go into this process! While they are learning responsibility, they are also practicing their executive functioning skills!

To some teachers, teaching kids when and how to transition from one activity to the next seems trivial. To me, it's an important part of teaching my students to understand how to maximize the time that we spend learning in our class. Over time, students learn how many minutes are needed for each transition and begin to call, "Give Me Fives!" when it's time to transition. If they get it wrong, students politely correct them by saying, "We don't have very much to do before lunch, so maybe we should wait another two minutes to transition." Even though my class is student-led, I want my students to lead similarly to how I would when directing our class—that's why we follow a detailed, daily schedule. I know, however, that certain students would use their power to transition the class earlier and earlier if they were allowed. I don't want that. I certainly would not tell my kids to clean up ten minutes before lunch! Imagine the amount of time that would be wasted during the course of a school year!

Since the schedule is on the monitor, students know what activities are lined up for the day. They can mentally prepare for things that vary from our typical schedule, which helps many of my students immensely. If they realize they've forgotten something for a lesson, they can make a phone call home. (I discourage my students from calling their parents often to bring in forgotten work because I don't want to perpetuate absent-mindedness by enabling them!) Our schedule can also build anticipation by getting students to talk about exciting lessons with their peers at non-instructional times.

WEEKLY SCHEDULE

Displaying a schedule takes the anxiety out of the day for so many students. One of the best outcomes of displaying the schedule and having clearly defined transition times is that students who have not been leaders in previous years have countless opportunities to lead! Anytime they notice it's around the right time to move from one activity to the next, they generally feel comfortable doing the "Give Me Five!" and starting the transition. Immediately after their announcement, another child may call another "Give Me Five!" and add an important piece to the previous direction like, "Don't forget to move the tables back; yesterday I had to do it by myself because we forgot!" This is collaboration in action, and it is student-directed, not teacher-directed. My students run the classroom because they've been empowered and have been taught the skills to do so.

DISPLAYING A SCHEDULE TAKES THE ANXIETY OUT OF THE DAY FOR SO MANY STUDENTS.

Early in the school year, I tell my students I will be testing their abilities to get started without a teacher quite often. I may not be in the classroom at certain times, or I might not show up at Music to bring them back to class. These are opportunities for students to show me that they can make collaborative decisions without conflict and follow their peers' lead without needing to be in charge. I let them know I will be watching and will have other teachers watching. When they show me they can consistently handle experiences like this, my students (and I) earn a Silent Day. (*Ooooh, ahhhh!*)

SILENT DAY

Silent Day is pretty special. From the moment the bell rings at 9:05, to the moment it rings again at 3:35, I cannot say a word to *anyone*! I can't speak to my peers at lunch. I can't answer questions. I can't say, "Bless you" when someone sneezes. (I messed that up once. Whoops!) Emergencies are the only exception to the silence rule.

My students are required to run the entire day without any guidance from me. They have to pretend I am absent, so they can't ask me to go to the bathroom or affirm any of their decisions. They need to get along, stay focused, make decisions, and have a full, typical

COLLABORATIVE COURTESY

Several times a day, students leave the room for various reasons. My students are empowered to pick up documents from the printer, take a book to the library, or make a copy of a worksheet. If my students are leaving the room for a reason that might benefit others, they are to do a "Give Me Five" and ask if anyone else needs anything copied or returned to the library. Not only is the practice a basic courtesy, it prevents several students from going places together, unsupervised, to do the exact same task. This way, the other students can get back to work, while one student runs the errand. I make sure these errands are not dominated by one student, so everyone maximizes their time on task. Although these short, quick interruptions may seem distracting at first, eventually everyone comes to appreciate their collaborative spirit. And because "Give Me Fives" are so common in our classroom, students quickly recover from the short, direct distractions.

day of school—with-out the direction of an adult. (Of course, for legal reasons, I stay in the classroom and observe, but I try my best to stay out of their business.)

I always plan for a Silent Day to happen towards the end of the year when my students are most confident, know all of our rituals, and have worked out most of the kinks. Also, I always have it on a math test day, so no math instruction is needed. Students pass out the prepared exams and one of them says what I normally say before a test:

> *"I want everyone to try their best, but you know I'd rather you all fail than cheat, because I can always help you re-learn the material, but I can't turn back time and give you back the trust that I lost. Please read all of the directions carefully and look over your test before you turn it in."*

Since I'm not available to answer questions during the test, my students do a "Give Me Five" and ask the whole class their questions. They know not to ask or say things that would give away an answer. The first time a student called a "Give Me Five" during a test, I struggled to keep silent. Tests are quiet moments and a student was shouting out to the whole class! Once I knew what they were asking the class, relief and pride replaced my momentary fear. I actually found it impressive that the student thought of a solution and had the guts to ask for help!

Before my first Silent Day, I was sure there would be problems. My guess was that there would be:

- arguments,
- power struggles between peers,
- students taking advantage of the lack of supervision,
- students not trying very hard,
- students asking me questions,
- students acting silly.

But, the only real problem I've had is that some of my most distractible kids have had trouble focusing and don't get much work done. Fortunately, most of the time, their peers ignore their off-task behavior and stay focused on what they need to accomplish. Many will even help the child re-focus and get back on track. That said, last year I had seven students with ADD. Not one of them got off-task all day! (Although, I did have one other student have some trouble focusing.) These students rose to the challenge and were completely successful, probably due to the novelty of the day and the amount of trust that went into it! I videotape the day from each of our classroom computers and watch the video the next day in order to give them feedback. (Students know they are being filmed; I don't use spy cameras!)

"My daughter was so excited about Silent Day. It was like a big race they were all training for, and race day was coming up. They had been preparing for weeks and were nervously excited to take on such a big responsibility. The day went smoothly—and the students were so proud of themselves. Best of all, they had fun and did exactly what they were supposed to do. The day wasn't so much about academics as it was about responsibility, self-confidence, and teamwork. Those life skills are so important at this age and so difficult to teach."

—*Jamie Bartosch, Parent*

All year long, my students practice to earn the privilege of a Silent Day. They know they can't earn it without taking responsibility for their actions and seeing that all the necessary tasks get done each day. Providing students with ample opportunities to lead and teaching them processes and skills, such as time-management and focus, helps prepare them for this special day—and for life beyond the classroom.

ENSURING EVERYONE GETS A CHANCE TO LEAD

Sometimes, creating a "student-led classroom" can turn into a "Becky-run classroom" or an "Anthony-run classroom." What I mean by that is, sometimes one or two students want to take on *all* the responsibilities, rush to do *all* of the collaborative responsibilities, and end up *becoming* the teacher. This is bad for the student, and it's bad for the collaborative nature of the classroom! In effect, the teacher has just traded places with the student; nothing else has changed.

To create a classroom full of leaders, rather than just a handful of bosses, my students and I discuss this phenomenon at a classroom meeting early in the year. The meeting helps prepare students with a course of action if and when student leaders turn into student bosses. I suggest my students use metacognition (thinking about their thinking) to assess and address this issue in *themselves* before it becomes a problem. To prevent tension between students, I assure my class that student "teachers" won't be allowed to get out of hand. I want them to understand that their responsibility in this particular area is for their *own* actions; it's my job to correct their peers' leadership skills.

In addition, I ask my students to spread the wealth and allow others the chance to complete tasks they have already done. I also ask them to identify and suggest tasks that need to be done. Polite suggestions from peers often encourage students to attempt things like "Give Me Fives" or to go into closets to get supplies for the first time. These are things some students feel nervous to do without a gentle nudge. And who better to nudge them than a respected peer?

This type of collaborative guidance promotes leadership within the classroom, so overeager students don't take away opportunities from children who are not as quick to identify tasks that need to be done. Teach students that a sign of leadership and maturity is encouraging others to become more active leaders. Instead of getting "credit" for being a leader, great leaders give credit to someone else. This can be so hard for children to do because they are naturally competitive with their peers. But our classroom isn't about individual victories; it's about collaborative ones. If everyone isn't successful, then no one is successful!

OUR CLASSROOM ISN'T ABOUT INDIVIDUAL VICTORIES; IT'S ABOUT COLLABORATIVE ONES.

One child's excessive enthusiasm can have a negative impact on the success of the whole class. If students just can't stop themselves from running to the phone to answer it first, or staring at the clock to do their "Give me five" before everyone else, then a one-on-one discussion is necessary. Affirm these eager leaders that you're proud of their desire to lead, and remind them that they *must* allow others opportunities to lead as well. Occasionally, if students won't stop or can't seem to help themselves, I temporarily take away their "powers" until I feel they can handle the responsibility of sharing the leadership opportunities. A few weeks to a month usually improves the situation.

Preventing individual students from dominating the leadership opportunities isn't the only way to increase student leadership. Creating a familiar format for reoccurring activities helps students anticipate exactly what needs to be done and how to do each task. That's why rituals are an important aspect of student-led classrooms.

"Mr. Solarz created an atmosphere of confidence in his room. The expectation in the room became responsibility, independence, and a sense of ownership of one's work. Pride in accomplishment...one of the best life lessons!"

—*Emily Goodwin, Parent*

USING RITUALS TO ENCOURAGE RESPONSIBILITY

As the students file into the classroom after recess on Monday, one calls out, "It's time for Lit Circles. Take out your books, get your iPads, and move the tables!" Everyone loves Literature Circles, so the students happily oblige. (See "Literature Circles" on page 132.) While I'm still wrapping up recess duty outside, my students go about the process of prepping the room for the next activity posted on our schedule. By the time I make it back to the classroom, my students are already reading together in small groups, discussing their books and recording their conversations.

Without any directions from an adult, learning is well under-way—something that wouldn't be possible if they had to wait for me to tell them what to do. The smooth transition happens because we have a student-led classroom, we have rituals in place, and students understand their individual and collective responsibil-ities. Promoting acts of leadership, creativity, collaboration, and reflection, our rituals provide structure and empower each student to lead.

A STRUCTURED ENVIRONMENT ALLOWS STUDENTS TO ANTICIPATE AND RESPOND TO THE CLASSROOM'S NEEDS.

Despite experiencing novel and exciting activities nearly every day in our classroom, my students are able to anticipate the daily flow. Our schedule is posted for all to see, and, for every reoccurring activity, we have a ritual to guide us through the process. So from walking through the door in the morning to going home when school ends, they know what to do, when to do it, and how it needs to be done. These rituals make it easy for students to lead; a structured environment allows students to anticipate and respond to the classroom's needs.

WHY RITUALS WORK

Rituals are activities that follow a similar pattern from day to day and week to week but are motivational in nature and are eagerly anticipated by the students. In contrast, *routines* follow a similar day-to-day pattern but lack the motivational element. Routines can even end up being activities that students prefer to avoid. Creating daily rituals that students are excited to lead is a key aspect of a student-run classroom. Knowing what's expected or needed often motivates them to take charge of the situation without being asked.

CENTERS/STATIONS

Some rituals are procedural and help our classroom operate smoothly. Others are curricular and take students through a process of learning. No matter the purpose, I work hard to teach each ritual, explain how students can lead it, and encourage them to take risks and make decisions on their own when new situations arise. (Remember not to overreact if they make a wrong decision. Provide corrective feedback without squelching their desire to lead.)

KNOWING WHAT'S EXPECTED OR NEEDED OFTEN MOTIVATES STUDENTS TO TAKE CHARGE.

We have many rituals throughout any given day, all of them 100 percent student-led. I get involved, only if I want to change the format of the day or the ritual itself. Although most of these activities can be led by anyone (or everyone) in the class, some rituals have specific students in charge. Even when a specific student is assigned a task, others know how to do it. That way, if a student is absent or if the task doesn't get done, anyone else can take charge. We *all* share *all* of the responsibilities. If one student neglects his or her job, we all share in the blame because we all could have helped. At the same time, however, I reinforce personal responsibility. Students kindly let one another know when we've done their job for them. They understand that, if they do another person's job for them on a regular basis, that person won't learn to become responsible.

At some point in the year, students stop announcing all of the directions, notice what everyone else is doing, and get ready on their own. This initiative reflects not only the power of rituals but also improvement in the students' observation and decision-making skills. Working independently, and without adult direction, they learn how to transfer these skills to other situations this year and beyond. I love how independent my students are and what great leaders they become!

RITUALS IN ACTION

In order for students to anticipate upcoming activities and transitions, our daily schedule is displayed on a TV monitor in the classroom. The schedule includes specific times for transitioning, lists the activity, and provides additional information if anything varies from the ordinary.

If you create rituals that students just can't become passionate about, they become routines. Routines have a negative impact on a student-led classroom because they drain energy and cause students to avoid them. Students are more likely to "accidentally forget" to lead the classroom when it comes to routines, and the teacher ends up taking on the responsibility. This detracts from the student-led environment you are working so hard to create. Convert these routines into rituals by making them opportunities for students to step up and accept a challenge!

For example, every morning when my students walk in the door, they go through a series of steps that are terribly boring and monotonous but necessary. For example, students must:

- Hang up their coats and backpacks,

- Take what they need out of their backpacks and put it in their desks,

- Move their lunch magnets on the Attendance Board.

GO AHEAD! TAKE A DAY OFF.

Teachers generally hate taking days off of school. Writing detailed plans for substitutes, hoping that the children learn what they're supposed to, and wishing that everyone behaves generally makes for a stressful day off! We're more likely to show up when we're sick, schedule doctor appointments on days off, and avoid joining district committees to avoid all the trouble of missing school.

That being said, when teachers create a student-led classroom environment in which students follow daily rituals, sub plans can be written quickly and the day practically runs itself! Since the teacher's role in a student-led classroom is mainly to observe, explain directions, and give feedback, substitutes are expected to do the same! On my days off, I schedule activities that students can run successfully without much direction from an adult.

They may be year-long rituals, like Passion Time and writing, or short-duration rituals we've practiced a few times, like preparing for a Reader's Theater (page 170) or Energy Debates (page 150).

Since my students have done these activities before, they know how to start them on their own, and, since they have been given directions previously, students know what needs to get done and are comfortable solving problems on their own. Quite often, I come back to proudly discover that one or more students taught mini-lessons to the class on their own!

The comments I shared in Chapter 2 are indicative of how substitute teachers react to students who know how to appropriately and respectfully take charge of the classroom. Most are extremely impressed! They often comment that the students directed their own learning and that they collaborated well all day. Of course, they also typically state that my students were chatty and energetic; but that's just how we roll.

When I return to school the next day, I'm always so proud of my students, and I'm equally impressed by the substitutes who were not too intimidated to let twenty-seven ten-year-olds run the classroom. What brave souls!

These steps could become a boring routine that kids forget or half-heartedly complete. So why not create a process that enlists a few students to help coordinate the steps and assist other students? Turn routines into rituals that get kids involved. Even when you assign jobs, rituals get taken care of by the collective whole because students have passion for rituals. Instead of going through the motions, my "Morning Greeter" happily says good morning to those entering the room, reminds them to move their lunch magnet, and tells them what our whole-class goal is for the day. The Attendance Takers look over the magnet board and remind those who haven't yet moved their lunch magnet to do so, tally the numbers, and submit our lunch count and attendance electronically. All of these essential tasks are being done while I am greeting my students, listening to personal stories, sharing a laugh, and creating a stronger bond with each individual entering the room.

Using rituals involves students with important processes in our room and keeps me from being consumed by the necessary busywork. Equally important, rituals encourage students to interact with and support one another. It's a win-win solution!

SIMPLIFY WITH PROCEDURAL RITUALS

Procedural rituals help the classroom run smoothly without teacher support. Here are a few ways I ensure students know what to do for each of the day's lessons:

- Activities on the daily schedule are color-coded, so students know if they need computers (red text), iPads (purple text), or no technology (blue text).

- Our computer cart schedule is posted, so students know which computer cart we have checked out for the day. They can bring it to our room and return it at the end of the day.

- When the phone rings in our classroom, the student nearest the phone answers it by saying, "Mr. Solarz' classroom, student speaking!" Most of the time, the call is a message for another student and can be delivered without any interruption of my time.

- Math manipulatives and other materials and supplies are kept in consistent places and students are empowered to get their own materials when they need them (and put them away when they are done).

- Other than in Math, we are close to being a paperless classroom, but students have access to a copy machine in our hallway and a printer if they need it. I teach one student how to use the copier at the beginning of the year and they teach one another as they need it.

- Instead of requiring students to ask permission to go to the bathroom (and in lieu of using bathroom passes) I empower the students in my classroom to use a hand signal to let me know they want to go to the bathroom. They put their hand on top of their head and make eye contact with me. I nod to give them permission to leave the room. The silent signal is inconspicuous—and I don't have to hear "Can I go to the bathroom?" fifty times a day. It also allows me to keep track of who is gone and for how long (especially useful in case of a fire drill or other disaster drill).

- With rituals like these in place, I am free to work with students or give feedback instead of being bogged down by minutia. Now, if only I could teach them to answer my emails, do report cards, and plan lessons, I'd really have it made!

LITERATURE CIRCLES

I love teaching reading skills and helping my students develop a life-long love of reading. I've already mentioned our Shared Reading sessions. Another way we build reading, writing and comprehension skills is through Literature Circles. I originally learned about this small-group reading practice from Harvey "Smokey" Daniels at a workshop when I first became a teacher. After reading his book *Literature Circles: Voice and Choice in Book Clubs and Reading Groups*, I immediately implemented his ideas and have since adapted the activity to meet our class's needs and preferences.

I've already shared how students follow rituals to prepare the room for Literature Circles, but the processes don't stop with setup. Following consistent patterns throughout the activity helps students get more out of this valuable time. For an hour, three times per week, students read aloud in small groups and use rituals to increase comprehension and have meaningful discussions of the material. They share responsibilities and take turns writing summaries for each session.

CLASSROOM LIBRARY

During the past few years, I have collected hundreds of books from garage sales, library sales, discount bookstores, Scholastic points, and countless other places. An entire twenty-five-foot wall in my classroom is dedicated to a bookshelf I built to store this collection. The class library affords students dozens of choices of books for each round of Literature Circles. To make sure the books are "kid-approved," students evaluate every book they read. At the end of the year, those that receive low scores get donated.

In our classroom, Literature Circles are flexible groups of three to five students who are drawn to the same book, not by reading level, but by interest. Before each new round of Literature Circles begins, I ask the students to choose from ten different novels (all with a similar number of pages). I am intentional about selecting titles from several different genres. I also offer books that appeal to boys and girls, making sure that there are both male and female protagonists in some of the choices. The Lexile®, or reading level of each book varies quite a bit. Although I occasionally share the Lexiles with my students, those ratings matter little when students choose their books; interest trumps all!

In our version of Literature Circles, students read their entire book aloud in class. I feel that students get much more out of reading when they can bounce questions and thoughts off of their peers *while* they read. Since students are wondering things aloud, they are able to ask one another questions and use evidence from the text in a natural way.

One non-negotiable rule for Lit Circles is that students switch off every paragraph. I require this for several reasons:

1. It maintains students' attention better than switching off each page or whenever they want to switch (The Popcorn Method). If they drift off, their peers quite often recognize that they are struggling to keep up and can do something about it.

2. It teaches students about indenting and paragraphing. Students often have mini-arguments about where a paragraph starts and ends and practicing this every day helps them to see how a paragraph is structured.

3. Switching off more often than each paragraph (Each sentence? Each word?) becomes choppy and interferes with student comprehension.

During each round of Literature Circles, I give my students a digital bookmark with the minimum number of page numbers they need to read in order to stay on schedule. They are allowed to get

**DIGITAL
BOOKMARKS**

ahead as a group, but, if they fall behind, they are asked to catch up at home. If a group finishes their book before the other groups do, the students engage in alternative activities, such as acting out and recording scenes from the book, rewriting the ending of the book, or writing the beginning to a sequel.

DEVELOPING DISCUSSION AND SUMMARY SKILLS

Summarizing is a skill I believe students need to develop. To do this, I have my students create a shared Google Doc for each book they read. They take turns each evening writing a short summary for the day's reading. Since it is a once-per-week assignment, most students don't mind putting in a strong effort on their summaries. That

**LITERATURE
DISCUSSIONS**

said, students occasionally forget to do their summaries despite our end-of-the-day reminders. In those groups, responsibility becomes a goal they work on together. Especially early in the year, I review everyone's Google Docs often and leave comments, both with compliments and constructive criticism. This immediate feedback results in greater attention to detail and better discussions and summaries.

Discussions are one of the most important aspects of Literature Circles. They can range from simple "think alouds" by a student to formal discussions that get recorded and uploaded to our website. In a formal discussion, every student in the group must have contributed something new and intelligent to the discussion. As a class, we try to upload at least two formal discussions every day (more are encouraged).

I introduce formal discussions by teaching my students the six signposts as explained in the book *Notice & Note: Strategies for Close Reading* by Kylene Beers and Bob Probst. Those six signposts are as follows:

1. Contrasts and Contradictions
2. Aha! Moments
3. Tough Questions
4. Words of the Wiser
5. Again and Again
6. Memory Moments

NOTICE & NOTE

We first practice identifying these signposts during Shared Readings, so I can model the process and then listen and give immediate feedback as students make their initial attempts. As students identify signposts, they share them with the whole class, write them on a sticky note, and put them on our signposts bulletin board. Sometimes students mistakenly classify something in the story as a signpost when it isn't one, but Shared Reading is the perfect time and place to make those mistakes! It's just another example of students taking a risk and me being proud of their "failures." Once all misconceptions and misunderstandings of the terms and process are eliminated, students are ready to have independent discussions during Literature Circles—and a new ritual is established.

BY CREATING A FORMAT—A RITUAL—FOR LITERATURE CIRCLES, STUDENTS ARE ABLE TO GET MORE OUT OF THEIR READING TIME.

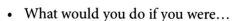

In addition to the six signposts, students keep track of the other kinds of discussions they are having about their books and write them on chart paper in the classroom. Conversation topics that frequently come up include:

- Dun, dun, dun! (When something is just about to happen in the book!)

- Predictions

- Connections

- I wonder...

- What if...

- Why do you think…

SIGNPOSTS

- What would you do if you were…

- Finding any behaviors from *The 7 Habits of Highly Effective People* in action

By creating a format—a ritual—for Literature Circles, students are able to get more out of their reading time. Knowing what to look for and how to keep track of their discussions and thoughts empowers

TEACHING CONCEPTS THROUGH MINI-LESSONS

Mini-lessons (five- to fifteen-minute segments) can be used to teach comprehension strategies and skills, elements of fiction, and figurative language. Rather than teach a concept in isolation, try to connect it to at least one group's reading for the day. Using relevant, real-time examples helps make ideas stick. As students are reading, they often come across confusing passages, new literary techniques, and unfamiliar vocabulary. These are perfect opportunities to do whole-class mini-lessons. If you listen in while students are reading and discussing the book, you will discover dozens of opportunities to explain concepts throughout a school year.

Whenever I want to teach my students a reading mini-lesson, I do so in the middle of the Literature Circles class period rather than at the beginning. This mini-break actually helps us make the most of our time. Since mini-lessons come in the middle of the period, students have already moved the tables, gotten the appropriate materials, accessed the necessary technology, and begun reading, all on their own because of the rituals that we have established. When I'm ready to teach, I call out "Give Me Five" and share the lesson. As soon as it's over, students can immediately resume reading and discussing their books.

them to learn and practice important concepts without a teacher's direction. And the summaries help me stay in tune with each group's needs and offer effective feedback that keeps them challenged and growing.

REARJMCL

Another example of a classroom ritual is REARJMCL (pronounced Rear-ji-mick-el). REARJMCL is our end-of-the-day ritual. It is when we write down our homework, evaluate our day, reflect on the goals we set for ourselves, and set new ones for tomorrow.

REARJMCL stands for:

- Recap

- Evaluate

- Announcements

- Reset the Room

- Do your Jobs

- Get your Mail

- Stack your Chair

- Line Up!

REARJMCL

This ritual takes about twenty minutes during the first half of the year and is shaved down to fifteen minutes by the second half. This is the last thing we do each day, and the entire ritual is completely student-led. As a matter of fact, I no longer have anything to do during this time other than observe!

As students transition from whatever activity we were doing before REARJMCL, the Recapper does a "Give Me Five" and tells the class to clear off their desks and take out their Assignment

Notebooks. Instead of telling the class what homework and responsibilities everyone has, they ask the class. As volunteers are called on, the Recapper writes each assignment on the board, the Google Calendar Kid types it onto our calendar (which is projected onto our board), and the students write it in their Assignment Notebooks. It is a requirement that everyone is silent during Recap because 1) the subject matter is important and 2) the end of the day is when students' attention spans are at their weakest.

After Recap, the Evaluator comes to the front of the room. I encourage students to sit as closely to the Evaluator as possible, due to the impending distraction of students getting ready for Safety Patrol. The Evaluator asks the class to identify specific things that were done well and were not done well today. Based on this discussion, we set one goal for the next day and write it on chart paper. Afterwards, the Evaluator leads a collaborative discussion to complete a survey that focuses on the goals that we have set for ourselves in the past (e.g. how we helped others, our behavior in Specials, if we remembered to do our jobs, get our mail and lunch bags, stack our chair, etc.). This daily review focuses our attention on our commitment to improvement over time. We discuss any problems, brainstorm solutions, and make it a goal to improve the next day.

With such a short time frame, the REARJMCL ritual follows a pretty rigid schedule. Recap begins at 3:15. Evaluate starts immediately afterwards. Safety Patrol can start getting ready at 3:27, but can't leave until 3:30. Announcements start after Evaluate but can't go past 3:30 because we need that time to do our jobs, get our mail, stack our chairs, reset the room, and line up! Students know these times by memory (they're not posted anywhere), remind one another, and follow them daily. The structure maintains order and empowers my students to have the confidence to do things without asking first. Since we all know Safety Patrol can leave at 3:30, my patrol students wave goodbye to me at 3:30 instead of asking if they can leave. This also marks the time when the rest of the class should be doing the remainder of REARJMCL (resetting the room, doing their jobs, getting their mail, stacking chairs, and lining up).

When the bell rings at 3:35, I give the rest of my students high fives and say goodbye. Many stop to chat, others prepare to stay for Homework Club, and some wait for their siblings to arrive. A lot goes on during the after-school transition! It's also an extremely important time for relationship-building for me and my students. Some kids may have gone through the day without saying a word to me. (I don't understand how it happens, but it does!) One of my goals is to ensure that I speak to each child at *least* once each day. Taking the time to say goodbye to each of my students ensures that I make a personal connection with each child every day.

ONE FINAL EXAMPLE

Let me go back to our morning classroom tasks as an example of how collaborative responsibility works in tandem with jobs and rituals. My students know certain tasks must be done every morning. I could assign one person to *do* every job. But that wouldn't encourage collaborative responsibility. Instead, those who've been assigned jobs, such as Attendance Takers or Morning Greeters, *remind* students of the tasks and collect information, but they don't hang up the kids' backpacks, move their magnets, or do their jobs for them.

If I left the morning routine up to chance, I would be dealing with trouble every morning. Things wouldn't get done! My students would likely prefer to chat with their friends rather than remind one another to move their magnets. Since I have assigned roles to ensure that each of those steps is taken care of, they get done. And since the whole class knows all of the morning tasks, if someone is absent, others step in and pick up the slack. That's collaborative responsibility.

Meanwhile, students have jobs to help everyone remember the steps that they may be forgetting. The Attendance Takers need magnets moved ASAP in order to submit our attendance by 9:05. In order to do the Pledge of Allegiance and hear our video announcements, someone has to turn on the projector and set up the computer.

The lesson here is that the operation of a classroom is the responsibility of the collective whole, rather than a specific individual. Setting the expectation that students can and should identify needs—beyond their assigned jobs—and respond appropriately provides them with daily opportunities to step up and lead. And that's so important!

Student Views on Responsibility

"In the past week my lit circles group could not figure out who should do the summary. We kept going back and forth on who should do it in class so after a minute, I said guys, I will do the summary right now so we can get back to reading quickly. I think I was using leader ship skills because I was saving time for my group and solved a problem." —*Stacy*

"Yesterday I had a boat load of homework,(in my opinion). I really wanted to try out making this one thing and did not know if I would have enough time. So I went straight to hammering down the homework and when I was done I was able to make plenty of what I wanted to do." —*Payton*

"We have to respect 'give me fives' and we have to be honest about things. These are important because if we don't respect the responsibilities no one has as much fun as they could while learning." —*Isabela*

"We have the responsibility to be a leader, help others and except help, get along with everybody, be prepared, share your ideas, follow instructions carefully, and respect everybody. I think that these are important because this is how to be successful in our class." —*Charlie*

Entrusting Your Students with More Responsibility

1. What tasks do you currently do that you know could be done by your students? How might you hand these tasks over to them?

2. Can you identify some "Collaborative Responsibilities" in your classroom that all students can share?

3. By the end of the year, do you think your students could be successful leading a "Silent Day"? If not, what can you change to ensure its success?

4. Why should collaborative classrooms avoid allowing individual students to take on too many responsibilities?

5. What daily or weekly activities in your classroom are routines? What activities are rituals?

6. What ritualistic activities can your students handle successfully without your assistance (both procedural and academic)? Would any of these academic rituals make good activities to do with a substitute?

7. Do you incorporate mini-lessons into your instruction? They are great for quick blasts of information or instructions! How will you encourage your students to present mini-lessons to the class?

Resources

[1] https://grantwiggins.wordpress.com/2012/01/11/transfer-as-the-point-of-education

Active Learning

*"The only source of knowledge
is experience."*

—Albert Einstein

We know students learn best by doing. Fortunately, the best learning method is also incredibly fun—for students *and* teachers! When students actively participate in class, they are more likely to take on leadership opportunities. A quiet room, or a room led by a teacher, doesn't promote student leadership, but an active, collaborative classroom does! It's great to see a class full of happy, engaged students working collaboratively and practicing new skills in

creative ways! An added perk of a predom-
inantly active learning environment is that
passive learning becomes more enjoyable
to students because it's rare. Students begin
to crave lectures and storytelling. They happily complete written assignments and work
silently when necessary because it's a novel
experience.

Scavenger Hunt

In this chapter, I'll describe several specific ways I create active
learning opportunities for my students. From history to science to
reading to communication skills, you can transform passive learning into active experiences your students will *remember*. Let these
ideas spark your thinking—I'm sure you can think of a dozen more
ways to create an environment suitable for student leadership and
active engagement!

STIMULATE THINKING WITH SIMULATIONS

What's easier to remember: something you've read in a book or
heard in a lecture or something you've experienced? Experiences,
of course! One reason students may struggle with history is that
lectures and books, even if they are interesting, don't always feel
relevant. But you can make this subject come alive by having students take on personas and participate in simulations that let them
experience history.

DON'T JUST TEACH LESSONS, CREATE EXPERIENCES!

—Dave Burgess, author of *Teach Like a PIRATE*

Before you start to worry that simulations might be too difficult or involved, let me give you a tip. Interact[1] is a company that has written and published dozens of simulations to help you provide opportunities for students to *experience* every subject rather than just read or hear lessons about

SIMULATIONS

them. This was my go-to source when I started doing simulations in my classroom. Once we started using this method, I was hooked! The excitement and drive in my students as they took on personas and worked toward learning goals convinced me it was worth it to invest the time to create simulations around all of my social studies units. (Of course, this teaching method can be used in other subjects as well.)

A REVOLUTIONARY EXPERIENCE

What if your students could travel back in time to 1776? In our Revolutionary War unit, that's exactly what my students do! As apprentices, they explore Boston and learn about America's conflicts with England firsthand. They meet different characters each day (played by me). Our very interesting conversations lead to research and discovery of historical events and different viewpoints.

For example, a character might ask one of my students: "It sure seems as though conflicts like this revolution we're having with King George can happen for so many reasons! What exactly led up to all of this? It sure seems like it was a bunch of things!"

THE REVOLUTIONARY WAR

WRITING SCRIPTS

When a question is presented, we pause the simulation so students can read a chapter in our textbook, hold a class discussion, or host an inquiry event in which students research the question with partners and attempt to answer it. Graphic organizers or outlines can be provided to help students focus their research and collect their thoughts. Students should be able to answer the question effectively before the class moves on with the simulation, but don't be afraid to continue, even if there is still some confusion about the answer. The class can hash out any misunderstandings in discussions with the character (you). You'll be surprised at how well students listen as you teach while staying in character!

Of course, our simulations are more than conversations between fictional characters. Students research their own occupations, create a collaborative Google Presentation, and use an app to create a timeline of events during our stay in Boston. They perform Reader's Theaters to illustrate some of the major events, like the Boston Tea Party and the Boston Massacre. We play a game of tug-of-war as a fun, physical metaphor for the war. And in addition to research-

HISTORICAL REENACTMENT

ing important leaders from this time period, we take a field trip to experience a Revolutionary War reenactment and speak to the reenactors about life during this time period.

One of my students' favorite activities during the simulation includes writing scripts for a partner and themselves. One character takes a Patriot's viewpoint and one takes the Loyalist's viewpoint on recent (1776) events. They then act out their skits in front of our green screen (complete with costumes I ordered online) and put in a backdrop of period Boston buildings (created on butcher paper by the kids). By the end of the unit, students are able to demonstrate a strong understanding of an event or two; they have worked collaboratively throughout the whole process and performed in front of a camera for the world to see! Aside from all the learning, it's a really fun experience!

LEARNING LAW IN OUTER SPACE

Once we've met the objectives for our Revolutionary War unit, it's time to blast off to Mars in order to learn more about our Constitution. What does Mars have to do with our Constitution, you might ask? Nothing! But this unique experience pro-vides the perfect backdrop for manufactur-

U.S. CONSTITUTION

ing conflict within a simulation. The simulation begins when my students are told they were the twenty-one (or twenty-five or twen-ty-nine) people selected by the International Space Community to be the first humans to set foot on Mars. Their job is to collabora-tively design and build a space colony where others will soon need to live, due to overcrowding on earth.

As a class, students brainstorm dozens of occupations that might be beneficial to the new colony. We then pare down the list to exactly the number of students we have in our class and pull sticks

We the People

to allow students to sign up for one occupation. This activity gets students to think several steps ahead and anticipate what kinds of people should be the first to head to the red planet. Later, we learn a little geography by announcing that this crew of ours consists of people from different countries around the world! Based on parameters I provide, they all choose a country, do some research on it, and create avatars of themselves on Voki[2]. With new identities, they introduce themselves to the world on their ePortfolios.

While traveling to Mars, students work together to create our new country and plan out what we will do once we get there. During this time, students are presented with various challenges intended to create conflict within the group. Ultimately, they decide rules and laws are necessary. That's when we discuss why countries have constitutions. We learn about our own Constitution, and after several lessons, students are tasked with collaboratively writing our colony's constitution on a shared Google Doc. If students decide to create a government similar to that of the United States, we divide our class into groups based on each part of the U.S. Constitution. One group researches the preambles of different countries and

Colonize Mars

writes one for our country. One group writes a Bill of Rights, based on the U.S. Bill of Rights. The other groups write sections, based on our legislative, judicial, and executive branches. If they choose not to model their constitution on ours, they determine how they will divide up the responsibilities. Either way, we ultimately end up with an amazing Constitution, written by the kids for the kids who live on Mars. My students always feel so proud when they finish this activity!

WESTWARD EXPANSION

FROM MARTIAN PIONEER TO WESTWARD PIONEER

Shortly after we've created our Martian government, an emergency forces us to leave the planet quickly. When we arrive back home, something strange has happened: We've landed in Independence, Missouri, in 1843, and Conestoga wagons are everywhere. Newspapers report that aliens have landed (us) and are confusing the pioneers! We have to find ways to solve the problems that come with being in a strange place with no money and no knowledge of what's going on! Fortunately for us (and unfortunately for him), our space ship landed on a gold miner who happened to be holding a bag of gold.

Our money problem is solved, but we have to figure out the rest of the story. We decide to join the pioneers heading west along the Oregon Trail, so we purchase wagons and oxen and supplies and head westward. Students are faced with many challenges in this simulation and are asked to find solutions. They conduct research for an authentic purpose, use critical thinking skills, and cite their evidence to convince the group to choose their solution. Based on the class's decision, good or bad consequences come their way.

OREGON TRAIL

At the end of each daily experience, students participate in creative reflection activities that get them to explain what happened, what the group decided, and the results of that decision. These activities include making videos, taking posed photographs, contributing to various web tools, and even collaboratively writing an unrealistic fiction story. Although I play an important part in the facilitation of these lessons, the students take ownership of the problem-solving and reflection portions and display great leadership skills while collaborating with one another. Students rave about how much fun each experience is, and I'm meeting all of my objectives, Essential Questions, and Common Core standards along the way!

I've found that students enjoy learning the content so much more when they are actively involved in the setting of the story. By becoming fictional characters, learning alongside actual historical figures, witnessing events in history, and standing where others have stood before us, students learn the content in a more permanent way. It's hard to forget how the Boston Massacre started when you were personally responsible for throwing snowballs at British soldiers. It's hard to forget that we, as citizens of the United States (and Lopistan, as our Martian colony was called last year) have certain rights that cannot be usurped when we brainstormed and negotiated to make those rights our own. It's hard to forget all the problems pioneers experienced on their journey west, when we got swindled by a snake-oil salesman and nearly died from dysentery.

Experiences make learning memorable. I encourage you to provide as many simulated opportunities as you can for your kiddos. They'll appreciate it for years to come!

DEVELOPING DEEPER UNDERSTANDING WITH DEBATES

Although competition can have a negative impact on collaboration, I see tremendous value in debates, when set up properly. Debates are a fun way to get students researching, planning, and speaking in front of others. Bonus: Student engagement and motivation skyrocket during all stages of our debates.

The Alternative Energy Debates are introduced by *President Solarz* in a conference with his *advisors*. My advisors (students) are asked to research alternative energy sources that would help our country minimize its reliance on fossil fuels. As president, I commit to investing all of our country's energy dollars in the winning energy group's source.

STUDENT ENGAGEMENT AND MOTIVATION SKYROCKET DURING ALL STAGES OF OUR DEBATES.

Ahead of time, students are placed into mixed-ability groups of three to four students. I pull sticks and allow the groups to choose which of the six to eight energy sources they'll be lobbying for. During the following weeks, I conduct mini-lessons for the whole class and assign tasks to each group with deadlines for completion. Students may divide the workload, but they must work in the same area and rely on one another for help when needed. As soon as one group has completed the

ENERGY DEBATES

151

first task, I introduce the next to the entire class and everyone completes it when they are ready. Overlapping assignments, rather than making a group wait until everyone has finished, keeps the class moving and prevents complacency.

The first task is to research their energy source. The main energy sources we usually work with include nuclear, wind, solar, geothermal, hydropower, biomass, and tidal/wave power. (We avoid fossil fuels because one of our purposes is to replace them for environmental reasons.) I provide each group with a small packet of basic information to get them started, but they are responsible for conducting online research for the rest of what they need. To guide their research, I provide each group with a short list of broad questions. Some of the questions include:

- How does your energy source get converted into electricity?
- How available is your energy source? Can people use it anywhere in the world?
- How expensive is your energy source? Does it cost so much that energy companies avoid using it?
- How much does your energy source pollute or destroy the environment?
- What are the pros and cons of your energy source?

The next task is to organize their learning by creating a large, ten-foot by three-foot poster with the answers to the questions displayed in a visually appealing way. While some groups are starting their poster, other groups are still completing their research. Groups are required to check in before they're allowed to get their poster paper. When the first group finishes its poster, it's time to introduce the next task: preparing a defense. The first activity helped groups identify several cons about their energy source. Now it's time to focus on finding ways to defend their energy sources against those arguments. In addition to writing formal responses, they are also encouraged to find photos and videos to help support their defenses during the debate. An example of a defense would be:

> *"Yes, it's true. Coal energy pollutes, but scientists have improved technology so much that scrubbers are removing up to 95 percent of the sulfur dioxide produced in the process of burning coal, according to website A."*

When students are able to accept the criticism against their energy source, and spin it in a way that makes their source look better, they are learning the art of persuasion and argumentation. I also teach them the importance of not lying, exaggerating, or providing misinformation during this step. To keep everyone honest, I act as the fact-checker and point out incorrect information to the judges at breaks during the actual debate.

When students can't identify any more cons, I announce pairings for the first round of debates. At this point, students research their opponent's energy source and write arguments against them. Before a group moves on to the next step, its members must organize their arguments from strongest to weakest and try to eliminate any overlapping arguments. This important step in the process teaches analysis and evaluation skills.

EVALUATION

Again, they are encouraged to find photos and videos that help to clarify the argument for the other team and make it more

**DEBATE
PREPARATION**

meaningful to the judges. Through this practice, students learn the value of visuals. For example, one group used an extremely powerful video to show how wind turbines frequently injure and kill birds. The video showed a bird getting hit by a moving wind turbine. The visual explanation made such an impact that the group was able to knock their opponent out of the round!

Next, students begin writing their opening statements (persuasive or argumentative essays). For years, I taught a unit on how to write a persuasive-style essay, but the method felt kind of boring and my students' writing skills didn't advance as much as I would have liked. To improve the writing unit, I integrated it with our Alternative Energy Debates. Learning that a strong persuasive essay could sway the judges during the debate *and* earn them enough points to win a round, motivated my students to do their very best (one of the positive effects of competition). Suddenly, they *wanted* to learn the tips, tricks, and persuasive writing techniques. Better yet, they used them in their essays to support their alternative energy source. Later, I added an online, graphic organizer[3] to the unit, a tool that utilized my tips and tricks and allowed students to work collaboratively in real time. The organizer helped them craft stronger arguments that were well-thought-out and more fully-supported. Because they worked collaboratively, three or four students had input into the essay instead of just one, which resulted in even better writing. Prior to using the technology, I had one student writing, while the others contributed. But with all four typing information into the organizer while discussing it out loud, everyone was fully-engaged in the process. It was true collaboration at work!

Once everyone completes their opening statements (persuasive/argumentative essays), it's time for Round 1 of the Alternative Energy Debates! Every group participates in Round 1, but only two at a time. The winners of Round 1 move on to Round 2 (or sometimes Round 3 if they get a "Bye" in Round 2 due to numbers). Students not currently debating act as judges. They are asked to bring a pencil and paper and are taught to keep tallies when groups make strong arguments or defenses. Prior to starting, I lead a discussion about honest judging and the importance of voting fairly for each team. No favoritism or special treatment is allowed.

During the debate, one student is in charge of the online stopwatch[4]. Every group gets one minute to make an argument and one minute to defend, but they can take longer if they are using visuals. Opening statements and closing remarks have no time limit. During the debate, students present arguments and defend their positions. To keep it courteous, students say things like, "I respectfully disagree with our opponents" and "Our esteemed judges..."

ALTHOUGH DEBATES ARE COMPETITIVE, STUDENTS ARE CONSTANTLY COLLABORATING WITHIN THEIR GROUP.

When the arguments and defenses phase ends, each team goes into the hallway and writes their closing remarks. Closing statements offer an opportunity to argue points made by the other team that they thought were incorrect or exaggerated. They may also re-state

DEBATE VIDEOS

any points they want the judges to really remember. While the groups write their closing statements, I chat with the judges about any misinformation provided in the arguments, though I am careful not to sway opinions in any way. Judges are not allowed to talk about the debate at all during this time, to prevent influencing one another. Finally, the two groups come in and present their closing remarks. Afterwards, I escort them back to the hallway, while the judges cast their silent votes and I break any ties. (I never tell students the final vote, whether it was a tie, close call or a runaway.) I bring the groups back in and we announce a winner. Prior to hearing the decision, students are instructed on how to congratulate the other team and how to react when hearing the winners being announced. Judges congratulate both teams, throw away their tallies, and are reminded not to talk about how they scored the debate.

The preparation process continues for Rounds 2 and 3. Students from the groups that have been eliminated from the competition work with me on enrichment activities related to Alternative Energy. A winner is announced after the final debate, and I transform once more into President Solarz. Expressing gratitude to my advisors, I announce my intention to dedicate $4.5 billion to further developing the winning energy source in America. (And the crowd roars with approval!)

Although debates are competitive, students are constantly collaborating within their group. Team-to-team collaboration is also encouraged when it comes to logistics and directions. Since I make sure to downplay the focus on winning, students learn to appreciate the fun nature of the activity and truly don't mind losing. The few exceptions of students who had a hard time dealing with defeat provided opportunities to point out the importance of learning and having fun, rather than competing and focusing on winning. Even when there is a clear winner and loser, I want students to know learning is a process, not a destination.

GETTING FASCINATED WITH FAIRS

SCIENCE FAIR

Why are Science Fairs becoming so old-fashioned when *inquiry* and Science, Technology, Engineering, and Math (STEM) are the buzzwords of the day? Why have many schools canceled them in favor of more teacher-directed science lessons? Shouldn't we be providing more opportunities for students to wonder, explore, experiment, and report their findings? I think so!

Students in my classroom regularly have time to explore interests of their own during Passion Time. (See page 215.) They may research their topic, conduct an experiment, build something— or do whatever they want—as long as their topic gets approved! They may even integrate the arts, video games, or music into their Passion Projects. Through experience, I've learned that, when children spend time exploring topics of interest to them during school, they become much more invested in the learning process. A Science Fair offers students the same benefit but focuses their attention on the sciences.

My class has been hosting an annual Science Fair for the past dozen or so years. I can't say I was always excited about making time for the event, but it always seemed valuable and worthwhile. So I kept it going. Today, I know why I felt compelled to continue the tradition. It wasn't just because I participated in them as a child and enjoyed it. It wasn't just because I saw my students explain a scientific discovery in a confident manner. I continued this tradition because Science Fairs are about inquiry at its finest! Students wonder about something and explore it! Science Fairs (and all fairs for that matter) provide yet another opportunity for students to direct their education and assist others in learning.

SCIENCE FAIRS ARE ABOUT INQUIRY AT ITS FINEST! STUDENTS WONDER ABOUT SOMETHING AND EXPLORE IT!

One challenge that has hurt Science Fairs in the past has been the fact that teachers have traditionally assigned them as homework; kids only presented their findings at the end. Not surprisingly, my class takes a different approach. The entire project must be done in school with me and the other students as their assistants. I offer to scrounge up most of the supplies, help with data collection, and be their gopher. Students secure time slots (using a student-managed sign-up sheet) to work on their projects before and after school, as well as at lunch recess.

All of the "paperwork" (we do ours on Google Slides) is completed in class, as a group. I walk students through the steps, a few each day, and give them time to work. Everyone helps one another complete their slides, and I give them both in-person and online feedback. Mini-deadlines keep everyone on schedule, and daily reminders during REARJMCL ensure that all are mindful of their assignments. Most students are able to finish their proj-ects during the class time, but some come

SCIENCE FAIR SLIDE SHOW

to Homework Club to tidy up loose ends. There's always a few who need a little extra support, which I'm happy to provide during Homework Club.

To begin the Inquiry Process, students look through Science Fair topic guides for something that sparks their interest. When they find a topic, I work with them one-on-one to fine-tune their Guiding Question. Since students are completely in charge of coming up with their area of interest, they are immediately engaged in the process and motivated to learn more!

I take my students through several steps designed to help them learn more about their topic (Review of Literature); predict what they think will happen during their experiment (Hypothesis); identify the components to change, measure, and maintain (Variables); and plan out how the experiment will happen (Procedure). These skills alone are extremely valuable and transferable, and worth the investment in time.

After those steps and a few more, we take a couple of months to perform the experiments. Everyone is expected to complete his or her entire Science Fair project, including the experiment, in class unless I receive a written request from a parent that it needs to be conducted at home (this often happens when projects involve pets).

By doing this entire project in school, I am creating an environment where students are expected to research, plan, write, and measure collaboratively with their peers. Parents and other adults don't have the opportunity to help their child, so each student's skills mature over time. I make sure to provide regular reminders about deadlines and teach mini-lessons so everyone knows what to do, but my students take it upon themselves to recruit helpers and "guinea pigs" to assist with their projects. It's really a wonderful thing!

Another perk of doing the entire Science Fair Project in school is that it allows me to oversee the process, provide feedback throughout, and discover what each student is truly capable of doing without adult interference. I absolutely love becoming their assistant during the experimenting phase and have learned that conducting an experiment together is a fantastic way to bond with students. One of my favorite, recent activities was breaking four types of wood with a weight being dropped from increasing heights in our gymnasium to see which wood was strongest. Breaking stuff (in the name of science) can be really fun! Plus, I now know which type of wood best handles impact!

While students conduct their experiments, they collect their findings on a self-made Data Table. Paper or electronic Data Tables work equally well, but we prefer to use Google Sheets for ours.

DATA TABLE

Students are instructed that only one variable can be changed within an experiment to ensure a fair test. This understanding is reflected while creating their Data Table. Creating these tables reinforces to students what their Dependent and Independent

Variables are, as well as their constant variables. They show how much change is happening (Dependent Variable) against what is being changed (Independent Variable).

During the experimentation stage in the Science Fair, students learn they need to be flexible. Although they write a formal procedure prior to experimenting, they must be willing to make changes to the process if needed to ensure the experiment works properly. No one should be forced to keep a procedure that isn't working! During one experiment, when a boy named Luke was testing different kinds of tape to see which one could hold the heaviest bucket of pennies, we learned that his procedure wasn't going to work. After a few trials, he knew he needed to make a change and restart the experiment. It turned out to be a valuable lesson in flexible thinking because the experiment continued without a hitch the rest of the way!

During these one-on-one experiences with my students, I let them make the decisions. But I also ask questions to determine their reasoning behind their decisions. At first, they doubt themselves, but soon they figure out that my questions help them clarify their thoughts and their confidence increases. It's a practice that helps them develop the thinking skills necessary to make informed decisions and verbalize their reasons to their peers. Ultimately, projects like these reinforce the importance of students leading their learning.

After the experimentation phase, we work as a class again to complete the project. In this phase, we analyze the data and prepare it for others to see. Students create graphs and their final displays. Graphs help other students see the subtle differences in each of the

SCIENCE FAIR PURPOSE

variables. The students' data is quantifiable, which removes some of the subjectivity. Tri-fold display boards show all of the important information, so observers can glean the important information quickly and efficiently.

Students also prepare an oral presentation to draw in people who are walking by during the Science Fair. Students are encouraged to begin with a hook, since the point of the presentation is to get people to want to learn more about their projects. Although my students don't think of it this way, they're writing a formal speech to be delivered over and over without memorizing it or using note cards, to an authentic audience. They are simply sharing something about which they are very knowledgeable in a way that interests others.

Each time they give their presentation, it changes a little—often for the better. This is revision in action! Because I want them to see how they improve over time, I have my students record their presentation the day before the Science Fair and again immediately after the Science Fair. The initial recording helps ensure they are prepared for the event, and it provides a baseline. The second recording is to show growth over time. They upload both videos to YouTube, embed them into one blog entry, and reflect on how their presentations changed. They are always amazed at how much better their second recording is compared to the first, and I make sure to point out that it's the perfect example of the benefits of revision. It's a powerful visual to help them understand the value of revising and improving their work.

I hope you will consider reinstating the Science Fair in your school. Feel free to dress it up and call it an "Inquiry Fair" or something else that makes it sound more progressive. Whatever you call it, you'll know what it really is: a great way for students to learn!

If a Science Fair isn't your thing, consider doing other kinds of fairs like History Fairs or Genius Hour Fairs. For example, instead of having students write biographies and reports about famous people, let them research and then "become" the person. They can dress like an author or character from history and act like them during a fair for parents, administrators, and the rest of the school to experience. Encourage the observers to ask questions of your students while they're in character. Some historians don't appreciate this practice because students may answer some questions incorrectly and misinform observers. But I know students get so much more out of an experience like this than they would out of writing a report or essay. The activity also builds their confidence for performing in front of others and teaches them to think on their feet. If you ask me, the benefits of this kind of active learning far outweigh any drawbacks.

DISCOVER THE POWER OF PROJECT-BASED LEARNING

Although I don't claim to be an expert in Project-Based Learning (PBL), I *am* an advocate. I strongly believe in the value of learning *through* projects, rather than learning about a subject and *then* doing a project. As has been stated throughout this book, students learn through creative and active experiences better than through passive ones. Therefore, creating projects that focus students' attention on content in exciting ways, providing them with choices, and allowing them to explore their interests are more effective teaching methods than lecturing or reading from a textbook.

Buck Institute for Education[5], my main source for PBL information, describes this method as one by which:

Students gain knowledge and skills by working for an extended period of time to investigate and respond to a complex question, problem, or challenge. Essential Elements of PBL include:

- *Significant Content—At its core, the project is focused on teaching students important knowledge and skills, derived from standards and key concepts at the heart of academic subjects.*

- *Twenty-First Century Competencies—Students build competencies valuable for today's world, such as problem solving, critical thinking, collaboration, communication, creativity, and innovation, which are explicitly taught and assessed.*

- *In-Depth Inquiry—Students are engaged in an extended, rigorous process of asking questions, using resources, and developing answers.*

- *Driving Question—Project work is focused by an open-ended question that students understand and find intriguing, which captures their task or frames their exploration.*

- *Need to Know—Students see the need to gain knowledge, understand concepts, and apply skills in order to answer the Driving Question and create project products, beginning with an Entry Event that generates interest and curiosity.*

- *Voice and Choice—Students are allowed to make some choices about the products to be created, how they work, and how they use their time, guided by the teacher and depending on age level and PBL experience.*

- *Critique and Revision—The project includes processes for students to give and receive feedback on the quality of their work, leading them to make revisions or conduct further inquiry.*

- *Public Audience—Students present their work to other people, beyond their classmates and teacher.*

Although I don't use every component listed above in every project, I do use all of them at some point in the year. Each is important for different reasons but can be difficult to fit into every project experience. After careful analysis of each component above, teachers should choose a few that fit well within a given project and try to hit as many of the other components as possible during the next experience. (You don't have to do it all at once!)

Project-Based Learning fits well in a student-led classroom. Students work independently because they know what they are working on. Mini-lessons can be taught to focus on content, procedures, or skills. And students feel comfortable collaborating with and helping one another solve their problems. Teachers have the freedom to observe, give feedback, and correct misconceptions immediately as they pop up. Students are actively learning, so discipline problems are generally non-existent and attention lapses are a thing of the past.

One project students complete in my classroom is called the Revolutionary War Hero Project. It looks completely old-fashioned (It's a poster!) and limits their creativity some (there are step-by-step directions), but there are aspects of the project that give students choices and are pretty creative! I have kept this project in the annual curriculum (with revisions) because it provides my students with an excellent opportunity to practice and display the leadership skills I want them to use on a daily basis. (And it's a perfect tie-in to our Revolutionary War simulation.)

REVOLUTIONARY WAR HERO PROJECT

For this project, students choose one Revolutionary War Hero from a long list of pre-selected people. Before they make their choice, I share a little bit about each of the people and/or allow time for students to research people they don't know. Next, students are given step-by-step instructions for creating a poster that includes several specific elements, like a "How to Be..." story, a medal acknowledging the hero's most important accomplishment, a backpack holding some of their possessions, and a travel brochure for people who want to go back in time to visit this hero.

Some upgrades I've made to this project over the years include using ThingLink.com and TubeChop.com to make fun, interactive presentations. Students start by recording themselves sharing all of the components of their finished poster project. They upload their video to YouTube and we use TubeChop to break the video into segments related to their poster's specific elements. Next, we take a picture of each poster, and use ThingLink to post tags on each element, which will take viewers to that segment's video. We then create a blog post with the ThingLink image embedded for others to see. The ThingLink tags allow people to watch a video on certain aspects of a student's project, without having to view the whole thing. Upgrades like these

INFUSING TECHNOLOGY

add novelty to simple projects and make the tasks more enjoyable for the kids—and for me!

Although each project is done individually, students do nearly all of their work in class. They work alone, but the room is filled with chatter because students are asking one another questions, sharing ideas, helping their peers with creative touches, and recording each other's speeches. This project provides an environment in which students can practice their leadership skills, as well as the other twenty-first century skills we work on all year.

Hopefully, you can think of ways to include more projects in your curriculum. Remember: completing projects in class helps make them successful. When students take work home, it can cause parents to become stressed. Very often, ownership gets away from the child. And if you're worried about having enough time to do all of this, I promise it's possible! Look at your schedule and make time by eliminating repetition in the curriculum, unnecessary lessons, and time wasters. Don't give more time than is necessary for lessons. Integrate subjects to improve your time-on-task. Use Essential Questions and Big Ideas to drive instruction, and rely on observation and feedback rather than regular summative assessments. By making changes like these, you can find the time to teach in ways that are interesting, engaging, and effective. Give this book to your administrators and have honest discussions with them about your thoughts. My hope isn't that you'll try to do exactly what I do but that these ideas will get your creative juices flowing and set you free to create experiences that help your students thrive.

Transformational Tech

Turning Up the Fun with Technology

As with the Revolutionary War Hero Project example, sometimes traditional activities can be spiced up by adding a technology component. Although I don't advocate using technology *only* for novelty purposes, it is a great way to turn passive learning into active learning. I encourage you to continually look for ways to use technology to transform what you are currently doing into something amazing! Think: What can I do with technology that I can't do without it?

In 2014, I received the Illinois Computing Educators (ICE) Educator of the Year award. It was a huge honor that focused a lot of attention on my use of technology in the classroom. The funny thing is, technology is not the main focus in my class. We use technology only when it's the best tool for the job. I never use technology for technology's sake!

Creating Campaign Ads

To be completely honest, four years before earning the award, I was one of the few teachers in our school who had never checked out the laptop cart. I brought my students to the computer lab only when lessons were created and led by others. I cringed at the thought of all of my students being confused at the same time and all raising their hands waiting for me to walk around and help them figure out their computer problem. But as I developed a student-led classroom and began to see the value technol-

PURPOSEFUL FIELD
TRIPS

ogy could add to my lessons, those fears faded. Because I knew my students would share the responsibility for helping one another, I decided to take the risk of checking out the computer cart. And sure enough, my students helped one another work through minor issues, leaving me free to help those with really tough problems. You see, it was my student-led classroom that allowed me to incorporate technology into my lessons.

USE TECHNOLOGY ONLY WHEN IT'S THE BEST TOOL FOR THE JOB.

For a long time, I felt that technology was a waste of time. After all, why should we spend six class periods having the kids peck at the keyboard, only to end up with a two-page, error-filled story about *SpongeBob SquarePants*? That's not a good use of time! Well, I've since learned that technology is not just for word processing. (Duh!) I've also learned that students' typing skills improve within weeks when we use technology every day for authentic purposes.

VOTING
INFOGRAPHIC

Now, when I plan units for an upcoming school year, I consider which technology tools might replace traditional tools. In addition to improving students typing skills, web tools can:

- allow multiple students to collaborate in real time to create graphic organizers or make graphs,

- enable students to revise their work

- transform a boring worksheet into a piece of art that students will be proud of for weeks to come,

- provide an authentic audience outside of the walls of our school,

- and create a stronger home-school connection.

Technology helps turn ordinary learning into extraordinary fun. And the whole time children are working with these technology tools, they are collaborating and helping each other problem-solve. Those results seem worthwhile to me!

ROLE PLAYING WITH READER'S THEATER

My students really love Reader's Theater! It doesn't really matter what the topic is or how much time they have to prepare, my students get excited about this activity. From the collaboration, to the autonomy they have to make it work, to creating props and costumes, they *love* Reader's Theater.

If you aren't familiar with Reader's Theater, think of it as a short play or skit. Students read their lines straight from the script while acting it out. The performance may include some props or costumes, but doesn't have to. The main purpose of

READER'S THEATER

Reader's Theater in our classroom is to increase our oral reading fluency. Students are expected to practice their lines for a few days, ask for help pronouncing difficult words, and learn to project their voice, add inflection, and enunciate. Connecting Reader's Theater to our curriculum integrates the skills they use into the material they're learning. (Are you sensing a theme? Active learning + integration + revision = unforgettable educational experiences.)

Here's a quick look at my process for Reader's Theater. First, I select a script with enough parts for my entire class and create sign-up sheets for each part. Then, I let the class know how many plays I need (usually two or three) so that each student gets a role. In an attempt to eliminate potential disappointment over parts or groups, I play up the benefits of each. I also try to mentally prepare them for the possibility of being picked towards the end when only a few parts are left.

I pull sticks and have my students come up to the sign-up sheets and write their names next to the role(s) that they prefer. They also write it in their notebooks so they don't forget who they are. They announce to the class who they have chosen, so others can prepare to make a new choice if their first was taken. (I have also used a shared Google Spreadsheet in place of sign-up sheets so everyone can see and enter their choice; it's worked well!)

Once everyone has their assignments, I explain that no one needs to memorize their lines; they each will have a script in their hands during the entire Reader's Theater. They will, however, need to become extremely familiar with their lines, so they can read them aloud fluently. They will read and practice their lines as a group, and they will need to read over their lines at home as well.

Then, I give clear directions to the class that they will be splitting into their various Reader's Theater groups and will need to complete each of the following steps in order.

1. Take a few minutes to look through the script and highlight all of your lines or actions.

2. As a group, read the script aloud, paying attention to all of the stage directions and other notes. Be kind to those who don't realize it's their turn. This is practice; no one is perfect! Feel free to share your thoughts or questions as you read.

3. When you are finished reading the script aloud, read it aloud again, and spend more energy trying to understand what is going on in each scene. Try to envision creative opportunities to make simple props and simple costumes that will help your audience understand what is happening. Take time to discuss ideas during this read-through.

Other important aspects of this activity include leadership and following skills. I urge students to freely share ideas and show appreciation for others' ideas. When being critical of ideas or making suggestions, it is to be done with kindness and respect. Students need to listen to one another's ideas and be willing to share their own.

For whatever reason, conflict always creeps up during Reader's Theater prep. I look forward to this as an opportunity for students to use their conflict management skills. I am always nearby, listening and watching, so, as soon as a disagreement starts, I'm there to see it. I smile. My body language is extremely calm. They look to me for help, but I offer none—at first. My hope is that someone will recommend using one of the strategies they've learned without a reminder from me. Usually someone speaks up, and I beam with pride! When they can't resolve the issue on their own, I do a "Give

Me Five" and lead a quick Classroom Meeting about the importance of remembering to use our conflict-management strategies. If the teacher is always willing to step in and handle conflict, then the students learn that they don't need to do it themselves! Therefore, I work very hard to demonstrate patience and confidence in my students' abilities to lead.

On our second day of rehearsals, students are asked to read through the play again as a group, but this time, they need to pause and create a to-do list of things that need to get done before the performance. When the entire play has been read through, students can break off into groups to complete those tasks. They will have one more period before the presentation to complete everything, including at least two "dress rehearsals." During these dress rehearsals, I occasionally give my input regarding props or costumes or actions if they don't seem appropriate or necessary.

On the day of the performance, we record the event and upload it to our YouTube channel, making sure to embed it in our Daily Photo Journal for parents to watch. I also offer some immediate feedback to the group to reinforce the skills they've learned and help them improve for the next time. I may ask my students in the audience to offer compliments at this time, but no criticisms.

By providing students with active learning experiences, such as simulations, projects, fairs and Reader's Theater, you set the stage for students to lead. You are providing them opportunities to think independently and to increase their collaboration skills and confidence. Since students are happier in an active learning environment, they take more responsibility for their education and enjoy passing on any new knowledge to their peers. I hope you'll give them a try in your classroom!

Student Views on Active Learning

"I have enjoyed wonder and energy debates. I have enjoyed wonder because I have always wanted to read that book but I never had the time. I would always be planing when I would read a book, literally I had a list with about 20 books on it! So when we got a chance to read Wonder I was so happy and when we had to go to lunch, I was one of the people going aw. For energy debates I loved them because I had a chance to learn about different types of energy types in a fun way. With all the jokes Mr.Solarz would say every often and all the slideshow and presentation making I had a blast." —*Payton*

"I enjoyed the energy debates. Because I have never done them before and they are are a amazing way of learning, also because we don't have to do tests in science when we are doing energy debates. It has been different because the way we learn is a different way then other teachers. Mr.Solarz has debates and fun ways of learning and other teachers would have just given us tests.Also I like passion time. I like it because I have only done it once and when I did it before we just did anything we wanted. But this year it is better because we want to work hard and we have to meet our deadlines and get everything done in a certain amount of time but we have fun learning about the topics we love." —*Emily*

ACTIVE LEARNING

1. What learning activities could you make more student-led?

2. Where might you identify opportunities in your curriculum to include debates, simulations, or projects where you currently don't have any?

3. During which activities can you envision getting your students out of their seats and working around the room collaboratively?

4. Active learning takes time. Often, teachers assign things like Science Fair projects as homework, impacting parents. How can you integrate active learning experiences into your classroom so students don't have to do much, if anything, at home?

5. How can you transfer some of the responsibility for content acquisition (research or otherwise) to your students?

6. Could Project-Based Learning (PBL) make a positive impact on engagement and motivation in your classroom? Describe one area of your curriculum where you can integrate PBL.

7. What project or task do your students currently do in your class that you can upgrade with some technology tools to encourage more collaboration, revision, or creativity?

Resources

[1] http://www.interact-simulations.com

[2] http://www.voki.com

[3] http://Creately.com

[4] http://www.online-stopwatch.com

[5] http://bie.org

Twenty-First
Century Skills

*"Children must be taught how to think,
not what to think."*

—Margaret Mead

For most of my career, I thought teaching content standards was my main job. I *had* to make sure they knew all of the parts of the water cycle and that America was an extreme underdog in the Revolutionary War. My students *had* to know that possessive nouns, contractions require apostrophes, and interrogative sentences must end with a question mark. Never mind that my students didn't know how to work as a member of a team or that they couldn't look

21ST CENTURY
TEACHING

up information online without help. Never mind that I sent children to middle school never having wondered about anything because teachers had always told them what to think about.

I knew something *had* to change if my students were going to develop skills they could use in middle school and beyond. I wanted to instill in them the ability to transfer their learning to new situations so they could be successful outside my classroom. I also wanted my students to look forward to coming to school! Was I crazy? After all, I didn't even like school as a kid. How was I supposed to make school so great they would *want* to come if given a choice? How could I, as Dave Burgess suggests in *Teach Like a PIRATE*, create a place so exciting that students would be willing to buy tickets to get in the room? Well, I had an idea.

I set out to identify the skills that businesses wished recent college graduates had learned before hiring them. I also looked at which skills colleges were asking high schools to focus on more. After a few days of online research, I had created a list with dozens of overlapping skills. I ranked them in order of how often they came up in my research. I discovered communication, collaboration, creative-thinking, problem-solving, and risk-taking were extremely important to businesses—and lacking in recent graduates.

I was determined to transform my class to allow students to focus on those skills more often… but how? I went back online and found an organization called Partnership for 21st Century Learning[1] (P21).

Wow! They had already done what I was setting out to do. They had already organized many of the skills into categories and identified observable behaviors to assist in assessment and teaching. One of the things I liked most about P21's framework (Figure 7-1) is that they point out the four C's most teachers consider twenty-first century skills: creativity and innovation, critical thinking and problem solving, communication, and collaboration. But they don't stop there. They go on to identify five key areas of life and career skills, as well as three areas of technology skills. All of these areas need more attention from teachers than has traditionally been the case.

After studying P21's resources, I turned my attention to Art Costa and Bena Kallick's *Habits of Mind* book series. The authors identify sixteen habits that can aid students in school and life as they encounter everyday challenges. These sixteen habits fit well into the twenty-first century skill structure I was developing for my students and complemented my existing content.

When I combined what I'd learned from P21 with the insights from *Habits of Mind* and my own ideas and experience, I ended up with a list of thirty-four skills in eleven categories: Communication and Collaboration, Creativity and Innovation, Critical Thinking and Problem Solving, Reflection and Awareness, Flexibility and Adaptability, Initiative and Self-direction, Social and Cross-cultural Skills, Productivity and Accountability, Leadership and Responsibility, Information Literacy, and Media Literacy. The following are the skills I want my students to practice in my class—and take with them when they move on.

COMMUNICATION

Figure 7-1

21st Century Student Outcomes and Support Systems

Learning and
Innovation Skills – 4Cs
*Critical thinking • Communication
Collaboration • Creativity*

Core Subjects – 3Rs
and 21st Century Themes

Life and
Career Skills

Information,
Media, and
Technology
Skills

Standards and
Assessments

Curriculum and Instruction

Professional Development

Learning Environments

Student Outcomes and Support Systems
Partnership for 21st Century Learning © 2009
www.p21.org/framework

COMMUNICATION AND COLLABORATION
COMMUNICATE CLEARLY

- Articulate thoughts and ideas effectively using oral, written, and nonverbal communication skills in a variety of forms and contexts.

- Listen effectively to decipher meaning, including knowledge, value, attitudes and intentions.

- Use communication for a range of purposes (e.g. to inform, instruct, motivate and persuade).

- Communicate effectively in all kinds of environments.

COLLABORATE WITH OTHERS

- Demonstrate ability to work effectively and respectfully with partners and small groups.

- Assume shared responsibility for collaborative work without dominating or letting others do all the work.
- Be sensitive to the needs of your peers and do what you can to help them.
- Use social skills in order to avoid conflict and maintain happiness.

THINK INTERDEPENDENTLY

- Exercise flexibility and willingness to be helpful in making necessary compromises to accomplish a common goal.
- Realize a group can accomplish more than an individual.
- Listen to and strongly consider the ideas of others.
- Leverage strengths of others to accomplish a common goal.
- Value the individual contributions made by each team member.

CREATIVITY AND INNOVATION
THINK CREATIVELY

- Use a wide range of idea creation techniques (such as brainstorming).
- Create new and worthwhile ideas (both incremental and radical concepts).
- Elaborate, refine, analyze and evaluate ideas in order to improve and maximize creative efforts.
- Conceive creative solutions to problems after examining various possibilities from many angles.
- Demonstrate originality and inventiveness in work and understand the real world limits to adopting new ideas.

WORK CREATIVELY WITH OTHERS

- Develop, implement and communicate new ideas to others effectively.
- Be open and responsive to new and diverse perspectives; incorporate group input and feedback into the work.

IMPLEMENT INNOVATIONS

- Generate tangible, useful, novel, original, clever or ingenious ideas, drawings, products, solutions, and techniques.
- Take innovations to the public (an authentic audience).

APPLY PAST KNOWLEDGE TO NEW SITUATIONS

- Make connections by referring to past experiences.
- Draw from experience when confronted with new and perplexing problems.
- Take meaning from one experience, carry it forth, and apply it in a new and novel situation.
- Recognize similarities between past experiences and current challenges and draw from what was learned.

CRITICAL THINKING AND PROBLEM SOLVING

THINK CRITICALLY

- Use various types of reasoning (inductive, deductive, etc.) as appropriate to the situation.
- Analyze how parts of a whole interact with each other to produce overall outcomes in complex systems.

MAKE JUDGMENTS AND DECISIONS

- Effectively analyze and evaluate evidence, arguments, claims, beliefs, and alternative points of view.
- Interpret information and draw conclusions based on the best analysis.

ASK QUESTIONS

- Ask questions to fill in the gaps between what is known and what is unknown.
- Ask questions at all levels of Bloom's Taxonomy of Thinking, but match the purpose with the correct type of question.
- Identify and ask significant questions that clarify various points of view and lead to better solutions.

SOLVE PROBLEMS

- Solve different kinds of non-familiar problems in both conventional and innovative ways.
- When appropriate, challenge yourself to find multiple correct ways to solve a problem.

REFLECTION AND AWARENESS
METACOGNITION (THINKING ABOUT OUR THINKING)

- Know what you know and know what you don't know.
- Know what to do and when to do it.
- Be conscious of the steps and strategies during the act of problem solving.

- Develop a plan of action, remember that plan over a period of time, then reflect back and evaluate the plan upon its completion.

- Be aware of one's actions and the effect of those actions on others and on the environment.

- Shift gears if a plan isn't working.

- Explain your thinking and the strategies used while making decisions.

REFLECT AND SYNTHESIZE

- Reflect critically on experiences in order to avoid repeating mistakes and to inform future progress.

- Synthesize and make connections between information and arguments.

- Identify those "Aha! Moments" when something finally clicks.

FLEXIBILITY AND ADAPTABILITY
ADAPT TO CHANGE

- Adapt to varied roles, jobs, responsibilities, schedules, and contexts.

- Work effectively in a climate of ambiguity and changing priorities.

THINK AND LEARN FLEXIBLY

- Change your mind when you receive additional data.

- Know when it is appropriate to be broad and global in your thinking and when a situation requires detailed precision.

- Understand there are multiple ways to solve a problem.

DEMONSTRATE LEARNING THROUGH ALL INTELLIGENCE PATHWAYS

- Interpersonal—understand other people.

- Intrapersonal—understand yourself.

- Logical-Mathematical—understand causal systems.

- Visual-Spatial—present the world in your mind.

- Verbal-Linguistic—use language to express yourself.

- Bodily-Kinesthetic—use your body as your media.

- Musical-Rhythmic—use music and patterns.

- Naturalist—discriminate among living things.

INITIATIVE AND SELF-DIRECTION
MANAGE GOALS AND TIME

- Set goals with tangible and intangible success criteria.

- Balance tactical (short-term) and strategic (long-term) goals.

- Utilize time and manage workload efficiently.

BE A RISK-TAKER

- Take educated risks and frequently push the boundaries of your perceived limits.

- Be resilient if your risk-taking isn't successful. Don't worry what others think.

- Know when risks are not worth taking.

- View failure as an opportunity to learn; understand that creativity and innovation are long-term, cyclical processes of small successes and frequent mistakes.

BE SELF-DIRECTED LEARNERS

- Go beyond what is required (the minimum) to explore and expand one's own learning and opportunities to gain expertise.

- Demonstrate initiative to advance skill levels towards a professional level.

- Demonstrate commitment to learning as a lifelong process.

- Work on tasks because of the challenges they present rather than the material rewards. Be intrinsically motivated.

PERSIST DESPITE SETBACKS

- Stick to the task until it is completed.

- Stay focused on your task without distraction.

- Have a repertoire of strategies to solve problems if one isn't working.

BE CURIOUS

- Wonder about things, then do something about it.

- Identify new problems that need to be solved and probe into their causes.

- Enjoy figuring out problems without adult assistance.

- Feel compelled, enthusiastic, and passionate about learning, inquiring, and mastering.

- If you can't figure something out, ask someone for help.

LEARN CONTINUOUSLY

- Value doubt rather than certainty.

- Explore alternatives rather than think there is just one correct answer.

- Constantly be on the lookout for new and better ways of doing things.

- Believe problems, situations, tensions, conflicts, and circumstances are valuable opportunities to learn.

- Invite the unknown, the creative, and the inspirational.

SOCIAL AND CROSS-CULTURAL SKILLS

INTERACT EFFECTIVELY WITH OTHERS

- Know when it is appropriate to listen and when to speak.

- Conduct yourself in a respectable, professional manner.

- Be humble, not a know-it-all.

WORK EFFECTIVELY IN DIVERSE TEAMS

- Respect cultural differences and work effectively with boys and girls from a range of social and cultural backgrounds.

- Respond open-mindedly to different ideas and values.

- Leverage social and cultural differences to create new ideas and increase both innovation and quality of work.

FIND HUMOR

- Perceive situations from an original and often interesting vantage point.

- Appreciate and understand others' humor.

- Be verbally playful when interacting with others.

- Be able to laugh at situations and yourself.

- Be able to turn embarrassment into laughter.

PRODUCTIVITY AND ACCOUNTABILITY
MANAGE ASSIGNED TASKS

- Set and meet goals, even in the face of obstacles and competing pressures.

- Prioritize, plan, and manage work to achieve the intended result.

- Be able to multi-task, handling many responsibilities at once.

- Double-check that everything is complete and all requirements have been met.

- Meet deadlines without reminders from adults and peers.

PRODUCE RESULTS

Demonstrate additional attributes associated with producing high quality products including the abilities to:

- Work positively and ethically.

- Manage time and projects effectively.

- Multi-task.

- Participate actively, as well as be reliable and punctual.

- Present oneself professionally and with proper etiquette.

- Collaborate and cooperate effectively with teams.

- Respect and appreciate team diversity.

- Be accountable for results.

- Seek feedback and respond positively to constructive criticism and setbacks.
- Attend to detail, precision, and orderly progressions.

LEADERSHIP AND RESPONSIBILITY
GUIDE AND LEAD OTHERS

- Use interpersonal and problem-solving skills to influence and guide others toward a goal.
- Inspire others to reach their very best via example and selflessness.
- Demonstrate integrity and ethical behavior in using influence and power.
- Know when to step back and let others lead.

BE RESPONSIBLE TO YOURSELF AND OTHERS

- Monitor, define, prioritize, and complete tasks without direct oversight.
- Act responsibly with the interests of the larger community in mind.
- Understand, negotiate, and balance diverse views and beliefs to reach workable solutions, particularly in multi-cultural environments.
- Perceive others' points of view, empathize, predict how others are thinking, and anticipate potential misunderstandings.

INFORMATION LITERACY
ACCESS AND EVALUATE INFORMATION

- Access information efficiently (time) and effectively (sources).

- Evaluate information critically and competently (use only trusted resources).

USE AND MANAGE INFORMATION

- Use information accurately and creatively for the issue or problem at hand.

- Manage the flow of information from a wide variety of sources.

- Apply a fundamental understanding of the ethical/legal issues surrounding the access and use of information (cite your sources).

MEDIA LITERACY
ANALYZE MEDIA

- Understand both how and why media messages are constructed and for what purposes.

- Utilize multiple media and technologies, and know how to judge their effectiveness as well as assess their impact.

- Examine how individuals interpret messages differently, how values and points of view are included or excluded, and how media can influence beliefs and behaviors.

CREATE MEDIA PRODUCTS

- Understand and utilize the most appropriate media creation tools, characteristics, and conventions.

- Understand and effectively utilize the most appropriate expressions and interpretations in diverse, multi-cultural environments.

- ICT (Information, Communications, and Technology) Literacy.

APPLY TECHNOLOGY EFFECTIVELY

- Use technology as a tool to research, organize, evaluate, and communicate information.

PRESIDENTIAL TRAITS

- Use digital technologies (computers, PDAs, media players, GPS, etc.), communication/ networking tools, and social networks appropriately to access, manage, integrate, evaluate, and create information to successfully function in a knowledge economy.

INFUSING TWENTY-FIRST CENTURY SKILLS INTO INSTRUCTION

Having thirty-four skills seemed excessive (and still does), but I believe strongly in each and have worked hard to infuse them into my daily instruction.

When teachers provide individualized feedback using twenty-first century skills as a means of teaching content, students develop actions and behaviors that are more transferable to the world outside of the classroom. For example, during the first week of school this year, my students were working on a science activity that required them to curate clipart images to portray the definitions of potential and kinetic energy. They gathered images of apples and batteries for potential energy and cars and cheetahs for kinetic energy. During the first few minutes of the lesson, I walked around the room clarifying directions, answering questions, and assisting students who were unsure of themselves. At the same time, I encouraged all of my students to be actively checking in with their neighbors to make sure they were clear on their responsibilities and offering help at all times. I reminded them never to leave anyone out and to get up and move around when offering help. This reminder reinforced collaboration and communication in my classroom, two very important twenty-first century skills.

With the activity underway, I watched over my students' shoulders to see how they were progressing. Some were off and running, while others moved pretty slowly. Believe it or not, I was more concerned with the ones who had quickly gathered a lot of images because I was worried they might have misconceptions or misunderstandings. I checked in with each of these students, asking them to defend their reasoning for their image choices. The questions made them think critically and evaluate their answers. Sometimes, they had solid reasons for their choices, and other times they couldn't explain why they placed an image in a particular category. One student understood kinetic energy well but thought everything that wasn't kinetic energy had to be considered potential energy. In response, I re-explained what potential energy was. Once she understood the concept, I asked her to do a "Give Me Five" and explain it to the class so everyone could benefit. She gladly did so. Although I prompted this "Give Me Five," it helped set the stage for future *Aha!* moments to be shared by other students.

WHEN YOU FOCUS YOUR FEEDBACK ON TWENTY-FIRST CENTURY SKILLS, STUDENTS FEEL LESS PRESSURE TO BE ACADEMICALLY PERFECT.

I try to keep several twenty-first century skills in mind whenever I'm walking around my classroom giving students feedback. In my opinion, these skills trump any other feedback. When you focus your feedback on twenty-first century skills, students feel less pressure to be academically perfect.. They know their teacher is looking for evidence of that twenty-first century skill in addition to academic skills. If a teacher's focus remains solely on the academic component, students are more likely to become competitive in the hopes of being recognized for their aptitude. And competition between students hurts collaboration, one of the foundational components of a student-led classroom.

THE IMPORTANCE OF REFLECTION

One of the most important skills my students work on is reflection. Although reflection, like many of the twenty-first century skills, isn't new, it deserves fresh attention. When teachers dedicate time and energy to the teaching, practicing, and assessing of reflection skills, incremental improvement becomes a way of life.

CREATING A 21ST CENTURY CLASS

Reflection isn't only for students. This important skill has helped make me a stronger teacher. Several years ago, I decided to work towards my National Board Certification. I'm not sure why I did it at the time; I think I just needed a challenge. Boy, was it ever a challenge! The assignments required me to write about my lessons and methods, and nearly everything required a follow-up sentence that explained the reason for choosing that method. The format required a tremendous amount of reflection and really caused me to analyze why I teach the way I do!

For students to make constant improvements to their actions and accomplishments, they need to learn how to analyze themselves and each other, identify weak areas, and make plans to improve. That's why we spend time every day reflecting on our actions individually and as a whole group. We set whole-class and individual goals and monitor our progress towards those goals. We devote time every week to reflect on goals that continue to be a challenge and discuss strategies for making progress.

One way I've transferred the concept of deep reflection to my students is by asking them to answer our ePortfolio reflection questions with at least two sentences: one must answer the question directly and one explains why they did it that way. At first, I thought this structure would seem rather gimmicky. I never liked assigning a specific number of pages for a writing assignment or saying they needed to write a certain number of words. To me, this felt like an extension of those regulations.

To my surprise, my students started to follow my request and their reflections were impressive. As with my National Boards assignments, my students wrote deeply reflective responses, and the introspection allowed them to learn about *themselves*. They uncovered misconceptions on their own and identified some of their personal strengths and weaknesses. They found new meaning in content that would have otherwise been lost in the past. A simple follow-up sentence to a reflection question created new learning within my students!

SYNTHESIS

Another way I have taught my students to write reflections is by following this step-by-step process:

Step 1: Describe what happened or what you did.

Step 2: Interpret how things went by using one (or more) of these sets of terms:

- Strengths and Weaknesses

- Successes and Setbacks

- Hard and Easy

Step 3: What have you learned due to this experience?

Step 4: Answer one (or more) of these questions:

- What can you do to improve your learning?

- How will you extend your learning past what is expected?

Reflection doesn't only happen in writing at the end of a learning process. In our class, students learn to be metacognitive in their thinking. Through interruptions in their learning process,

REFLECTING ON LEARNING

they develop an awareness of their progress at all times. I periodically ask them to answer questions about what they're thinking, assess their progress, identify potential struggles, and make plans for addressing those struggles.

After a few weeks of reminders from me to be aware of their thinking and decisions, my students begin to monitor their learning on their own. I slowly eliminate formal requests for reflection, especially during long-term assignments. I've discovered that, as my students begin to reflect on their own, requests for formal, written reflections during long-term projects reduce the chances that students will stop to reflect on their own.

I encourage you to teach your students how to reflect and be metacognitive on a daily basis, provide structure and support for them to do so regularly, and then slowly withdraw that support and see if your students continue to think reflectively. This practice encourages the act of transfer—the application of the skills you are teaching them to new situations.

TWENTY-FIRST CENTURY SKILLS PROGRESS REPORT

Evaluating skills through observation and feedback is an important part of the learning process. Because I place a high value on twenty-first century skills, I wanted to be sure they are included in a formal evaluation process. So, in addition to our standard

TEACHING REFLECTION

academic report card, I provide students and their parents with a twenty-first century skills progress report each grading period. Unlike our standard report card, this progress report does not use letter grades. Instead, skills are rated on a scale of one to ten and allow us to track growth over time.

The main purpose of this progress report is to help students self-assess and compare their beliefs with my observations. Based on our combined scores, students set goals for improvement.

During the self-assessment, I want to find out if students can identify their strengths and weaknesses. For example, does "Student A" know she is amazing at collaborating with others but really struggles to ask questions? Will "Student B" know he is a very self-directed learner but rarely applies past knowledge to new situations? Chances are, students don't know these things about themselves. That's why I feel so strongly about sharing my observations with them and making sure they understand what each skill means and what behaviors I am looking for.

After self-assessing and comparing their results to mine, students write up to five goals for themselves to focus on during the next trimester. We use the SMART Goal model[2] when writing our goals. Each letter in the SMART acronym stands for one of the five components of a goal: specific, measurable, attainable, realistic, and timely. Setting SMART goals ensures students don't bite off more than they can chew or set goals that can't actually be measured.

For example, "I want to do better with my capital letters" is a goal, but not a SMART goal. I teach them how to rewrite the goal so that it includes a measurable component and a deadline. A better-stated goal might be: "I will have fewer than three capitalization errors

**21ST CENTURY
ASSESSMENT**

on each of my writing assignments by February first." In regard to twenty-first century skills, my students might write, "I will catch myself taking on a leadership role at least three times by January fifteenth." Then sometime on or after January fifteenth, the student will reflect on his or her progress toward that goal and set a new one.

We set aside fifteen minutes every Wednesday at the end of the day to reflect on our class goals (from REARJMCL) and our individual goals. If we don't have a deadline coming up, we remind ourselves of our goals and focus on meeting those goals. If we do have an upcoming deadline, we start thinking of new goals to replace them. Or, we may re-write an existing goal that wasn't met and start formulating a new plan for achieving it.

If students can't come up with five goals that relate to either their academic report card or their twenty-first century skills progress report, then I offer to write the remaining ones. Of course, my preference is that they completely write their own goals because then they take ownership of them. Not all of my students choose beneficial goals, however, so I offer my assistance. Additionally, I encourage students, along with their parents, to write goals together at home to improve their study time and home life.

BECAUSE EVERYONE HAS DISCOVERED SOME WEAKNESSES, THIS ACTIVITY REVEALS THAT EVERYONE HAS ROOM FOR IMPROVEMENT.

Goals are set on the same day students receive their first report card and again when they receive their second report card. (We are on trimesters, so students get three report cards each year). We spend time analyzing our academic and twenty-first century skills report cards, which empowers them to explain what everything means to their parents. Their ability to explain the reports to their parents results in fewer questions and worries to discuss at conferences. Parents appreciate that their child knows their own strengths and weaknesses and like to hear they have a plan for tackling the weaknesses in the coming months. Their goals take so much pressure off of the parents and make the child more independent and responsible for their own learning.

Creating and going over progress reports with students takes quite a bit of time. Most of our afternoon on report card days is devoted to this activity. It can be extremely draining to be self-reflective to this degree! I regularly stop and thank students for their hard work and attention to detail as we review each component of the report cards. Even though it's challenging, I know our time is well-spent! Why would I spend so much time working on report cards and *not* make sure each child understands it completely? It's a process that provides the ultimate feedback opportunity. When we all leave for the day, we are all drained and have headaches from our intense thinking! And, we are all richer for the experience and ready to focus our attention on our goals when we return to school.

Because everyone has discovered some weaknesses, this activity reveals that *everyone* has room for improvement. Everyone sets the same number of goals. Everyone must continue to reflect on progress towards those goals. By the end of the school year, almost everyone has made strong gains in most areas. They enter middle school with more than knowledge of math, science, and social studies; they also have many of the skills necessary to succeed in the real world!

Erica and I just spent the morning eating chocolate chip pancakes and discussing her Twenty-first Century Skills Progress Report. WOW!!!! Once again you amaze me with your dedication to these kids. I absolutely love the detailed skills you chose to evaluate and reflect upon.... These skills are so valuable for Erica to work on and develop as she enters middle school and beyond! This must have taken you so much time! I appreciate it and thank you so much! We definitely came up with some more goals for Erica to work on, not only in the classroom, but at home. You are wonderful!!

—*Parent*

MAKING MATH (MORE) MEANINGFUL

I've contemplated changing the way I teach math dozens of times through the years. I've looked into Math Workshop, Guided Math, flipped instruction, online self-paced math sites, and Singapore Math. But for whatever reason, I have always come back to what I've always done. I'm not stuck in my ways. Nor am I afraid of taking on a big challenge. I stick with my method because 1) I enjoy it, and 2) my students make amazing progress each year according to all measures. From the outside looking in, my math class may look extremely traditional. But take a closer look and you'll see that dozens of twenty-first century skills are embedded into our everyday lessons. Here's a peek at how I incorporate valuable skills in our math period:

As students walk into the classroom for math, some choose to sit at our trapezoid tables and wait in line to have their homework checked by me. Although no grade is assigned to homework in our class, students take the practice seriously, and I provide feedback to ensure they feel their time and effort have been noticed. I look over everything they've done and give them feedback on everything I can. If they have a misconception, I re-teach it and ask them to redo a few problems on their own, while I start checking the next student's work. I continue to make my way through the line until I've seen everyone. I announce, "Last Call," when no one is left in line, to make sure I've given feedback to every student.

Every day, I give timely and personal feedback to each student. They process it, remember what they have been taught in the past, and combine it with what I am re-teaching them. This synthesis creates a stronger understanding, which makes learning more permanent. If students struggle one day, they are often motivated to try harder the following day. If they do well, their inner pride intrinsically rewards them and leads to sustained effort. They work hard for themselves and aren't driven by a need for praise or prizes.

While students wait to receive feedback, they work on the assignment I've written on the board. They are allowed to work with one another, and can ask anyone in the classroom questions, except for me. I am not available at this time because giving feedback takes priority.

These assignments are not busy-work. They are assignments that would normally be given as homework because the students have been taught the skill and need time to practice it. Whatever they are unable to finish in class becomes part of their homework, so there is incentive to stay focused and work hard on completing it correctly.

During this time, students make judgments and decisions independently, are self-directed, and are responsible for others and themselves. Some students work collaboratively and think interdependently. They use their problem-solving skills, working creatively with others as they ask and answer questions. Everyone uses critical-thinking skills and applies past knowledge to new situations in order to solve problems. Because the teacher is not available for questions, students must utilize their resources, persist, despite setbacks, and try new ways to solve problems because they know I will be looking over these assignments tomorrow. So that we finish in a timely manner, students set mini-goals for themselves and are intentional about managing their time.

When I am finished giving all children feedback on their homework and the previous day's classwork, it is time for me to teach a new skill or two, and my students are asked to take notes on the lesson. I strongly value the discussion that takes place between my students and me, which is why I have been hesitant to try flipping my instruction. During this time, students complete sample problems for me to see, and I make my decisions on whether or not to re-teach certain skills or, if they're ready, move on to the collaborative practice stage. I don't need everyone to be completely confident with the skill before moving on to the practice stage because I know my students will continue to teach one another, as long as there are enough who understand it. Going over the content until everyone understands it is futile. My stronger students would become bored, and my weaker students might just give up. By varying the way my students are being taught—both teacher-led and student-led—I'm providing them with a second opportunity to learn a given skill while maintaining their focus and confidence.

Students learn through a visual and auditory pathway by listening and watching my lecture. They also learn through a tactile pathway due to taking notes. I determine the pace of the lesson, based on the readiness of the class, so students learn continuously with little downtime. Students are asked to listen, learn, practice, and demonstrate their understanding in a psychologically-safe environment. During this time, confidence increases; students start the lesson confused and unsure of themselves but leave the lesson saying, "This is easy!"

Once instruction is complete and students are ready to practice the skills without my support, I ask them to return to their seats. I give them their classwork and homework and announce their partnerships for the period. Students are allowed to move around the room to work with their partners on the classwork. If they finish their classwork, they check in with me and can begin their homework, independently or collaboratively. If they don't finish their classwork, it often becomes homework.

Every day, during those final twenty minutes of math class, students practice problems together without my direct supervision. I walk around to check for understanding, give feedback, and differentiate based on the needs of my students, but they solve the problems without much interference from me. Nearly every day,

I remind my class of the importance of working collaboratively. When students disagree on an answer, a discussion takes place. If neither can convince the other that their answer is correct, they check in with another partnership, using me as a last resort. If they come to me, I often use this as an opportunity to re-teach and check for understanding for the whole class. This important time is where the real collaboration and communication take place! It's when students:

- Solve problems in partnerships, thinking interdependently and critically.

- Ask each other questions and learn how to answer them politely and clearly.

- Learn how to interact effectively with the diverse members of each partnership. They realize that, to get the task done, sometimes they need to lead and sometimes they need to follow.

- Learn to become responsible for themselves *and* their partner. Even though the teacher is available during this time, students are required to ask "Three Before Me." I will only help if the others around them cannot. This frees me to respond to the most difficult questions, which usually result in a quick, whole-class lesson.

With a few minutes left in the period, I ask the students to write down their homework in their Assignment Notebooks, and we start to transition to our next subject. Students learn independent responsibility by writing down their homework themselves. They learn to rely on a system that works for them for communicating to their "after-school self." By the end of the year (it takes the whole year for many of my kiddos), they have mastered a system they can use for middle school.

Since students have to write down their homework, put their materials into their backpacks, and get ready for the next lesson, they also learn how to be quick-thinking multitaskers.

If you walk into my classroom during a math lesson, you might not realize how many twenty-first century skills my students typically practice in a seventy-minute period! I don't turn on the projector, we generally don't use our iPads or laptops, and students take notes while I lecture! But now you know all of the twenty-first century skills my students are practicing. When they leave fifth grade, they are more prepared for the world, and math class was a vital component of that preparation.

GETTING STARTED IN MATH CLASS

During the first few lessons of the year, I explain how partnerships should work. Students learn that working together does not mean:

- Dividing the work.

- Giving each other the answers.

- Waiting for people to finish their work.

In our classroom, working in a partnership means students are:

- Doing the problems together,

- Discussing how they solve the problem,

- Discussing why they do the steps they do to solve the problem,

- Then comparing answers with each other.

Because I require students to work collaboratively, students who are struggling don't get past the first problem without someone explaining how to do it. They may need several re-teach opportunities before they really *get* the new skill, but they don't seem to mind if the teaching comes from their peers. I make sure to praise students for asking questions and seeking to understand, which reinforces the behavior and results in greater collaboration. Students often choose to work at the trapezoid tables, which is where I generally stay when I'm not walking around the room. Here, they feel comfortable checking in with me if they feel a little insecure or unsure of their math abilities.

Great collaboration doesn't just happen because I tell students to work in partnerships. To get buy-in, I've learned that students need to understand *why* I am so passionate about the process of working and learning together. Each year, I explain to my students, "If you're working together, you have more opportunities to get your questions explained in different ways, you have more people who will catch you doing *something* wrong before you do *everything* wrong, and you can combine your skills and knowledge to tackle more complex challenges!" It doesn't take long for them to comprehend why my mantra is "Two brains are better than one. "

PLANNING THE YEAR

Every summer, I begin with the end in mind when planning instruction for the next school year. I've been inspired by ideas and concepts in Grant Wiggins' and Jay McTighe's book *Understanding by Design (UbD),* which challenges teachers and administrators to identify what students need to know and be able to do by the end of each unit. Ideally, planning is done at the district level and tweaked by teachers to meet the needs of their students. With the final target in place, you then create assessments to measure students' progress towards those goals. Finally, you develop lessons with the end goal and milestones in mind. Beginning with the end in mind helps eliminate the repetition of lessons that, while enjoyable to teach, may not actually help students achieve the goals teachers set out to achieve.

In addition to ensuring that I'm working toward specific academic goals, *UbD* also helps me identify where I can naturally teach, practice, and assess twenty-first century skills. I start by reviewing my Year-Long Planner. On this grid, I list all the units, projects, and big activities we do in

21ST CENTURY SKILLS GRID

our class each year along the top row of a spreadsheet. Along the left-side column, I list the thirty-four skills I focus on in my class. To ensure adequate time is devoted to each skill over the course of the year, I mark an "X" wherever a skill is a natural fit. For example, our classroom Science Fair offers students a great opportunity to practice being self-directed and manage their time over a long-term project. Since everything gets done in school, students must learn to meet deadlines with minimal interference from adults. Additionally, the fair provides an opportunity to be curious about their world and find information and answers to their scientific questions through inquiry.

EVERY SUMMER, I BEGIN WITH THE END IN MIND WHEN PLANNING INSTRUCTION FOR THE NEXT SCHOOL YEAR.

Our energy debates are an excellent opportunity for students to work as a team and sharpen their communication and collaboration skills. They must make judgments and decisions on how to respond to arguments against them and learn how to prepare arguments and choose appropriate visuals and videos to use against their opponents.

For each unit, project, or event, I focus on specific skills when providing feedback to the teams or individual students. Although some students' results from their Science Fair project might occasionally be less than mind-blowing, knowing they worked on these twenty-first century skills makes the experience well worth the time spent! In addition, not every argument or defense during each round of the Energy Debate is 100 percent correct, but the skills my students develop while preparing and debating are far more valuable than the slight misunderstanding of the content. They will continue to learn the importance of accuracy as they grow older, but not everything has to be about perfection at this stage of their learning.

The way I've gone about teaching these skills has varied over the years. Most of the time, the skills are on my mind and are taught as they are needed. Sometimes, I begin a lesson with a short explanation of the skill. Sometimes, we do some role-playing or act out non-examples. Sometimes, we watch a video clip from a movie or commercial that shows the skill in action.

No matter what, I always make sure to find time to teach, practice, and give feedback on each skill every school year. These real-life skills are too important to neglect! The students who develop these twenty-first century skills are the ones who will become true leaders in your classroom. They will be the ones paving the way for the others with regard to taking risks and directing others. By focusing on these skills in your instruction and your feedback, you are empowering your students to use these skills in class. You are giving them permission to lead, perhaps even requiring that they lead. You are saying the content is important, but the learning process is essential, and *their* role in the process is vital.

STUDENT VIEWS ON TWENTY-FIRST CENTURY SKILLS

"During Lit. Circles, I usually lead the video discussion, but this time, I let Nicole do it. It felt nice to let someone else to do it. I also was letting others do the give me 5's." —*Johanna*

"My computers at home wasn't working at all because there were viruses in it. And I had to wait for a couple days but I was late to do it because I didn't know how to fix it. So I felt real bad so I quickly got my brothers laptop which was good and finished it I felt so good that I did it and I made it long and detailed and good and I didn't forget it. I made huge progress for making it long. I felt so excited!" —*Kaela*

"I couldn't sign in to google docs. I asked for help but they couldn't figure it out to. Then after 15 mins of trying to get in I realized I could change browsers. That worked and then I wasn't stressed anymore." —Madi

"I had a setback because everyone was asking me for help and I still had not started the reflection yet. I did want to help everybody but it was hard but I did help everyone who asked for help and I finished my reflection. At the end It felt good because I finished my requirements and helped everyone who needed it." —*Nicole*

TWENTY-FIRST CENTURY SKILLS

1. In what ways can you minimize your focus on content acquisition and increase your focus on twenty-first century skills?

2. During which activities can you imagine giving your students feedback on twenty-first century skills, rather than content understanding?

3. Which units or lessons would allow you to teach, practice, and improve a specific twenty-first century skill within it?

4. By the end of the year, on which twenty-first century skills do you hope your students will have made strong improvements? Why?

5. What can you do to encourage reflection after important learning activities to improve retention?

6. How often do you or your students set goals and track progress towards those goals? How can this become a more essential component of your instruction?

7. What can you do to plan units and activities that maximize your use of time and incorporate twenty-first century skills effectively?

RESOURCES

---

[1] Partnership for 21st Century Learning—http://www.p21.org.

[2] Bogue, Robert. "Use S.M.A.R.T. goals to launch management by objectives plan." http://www.techrepublic.com/article/use-smart-goals-to-launch-management-by-objectives-plan

EMPOWERMENT

"Recognizing power in another does not diminish your own."

—Joss Whedon

If you truly want your classroom to be student-led, I believe you need to make that goal explicitly clear from Day One. Students are prepared for anything on the first day of class. They're ready for you to be exactly like every other teacher they've ever had—or be completely different! Their understanding of and expectations for your classroom begin the moment they walk into your classroom on the first day of school. So go ahead! Jump in! Make a splash! Let them know this year is going to be different because *they're* in charge.

Embedded in everything you do during those first few weeks should be the idea that leadership and learning responsibilities belong to the students. Verbalize your intentions to your students; let them know you expect them to take charge of these tasks. Handing over control to the children you get paid to manage can be a scary concept! Some people (parents, administrators, and other teachers) may even question your sanity in making such a seemingly illogical decision. But pirates don't care what people think!

So, how do you get students to take control? It starts when you empower them to make decisions and address the entire class. Encourage them daily to use "Give Me Fives" to interrupt the class to ask questions, make suggestions, or share their insights. Provide them with opportunities to use their power every day. Practice will help them feel confident enough to run the classroom. In addition, be intentional about supporting any and all attempts at student leadership—especially those that fail. As I stated early on, they will make mistakes. (And so will you!) At times you'll need to correct students when they've tried unsuccessfully to direct the classroom. Do so with kindness and appreciation for their effort and initiative. Otherwise, students won't risk putting themselves out there! Help them understand that even failed attempts are preferred to passivity.

This entire book focuses on empowering your students to lead the class, but I wanted to dedicate a chapter to empowerment, because it must be a teacher's top priority. Many of the strategies I use to empower my students have already been explained in this book, such as "Give Me Five" (page 40), encouraging students to teach mini-lessons (page 225), teaching them the importance of roles during activities such as Mystery Skype (page 73), and letting them take charge of important classroom jobs (page 108) and activities such as REARJMCL (page 136), etc. Each of these teaching tactics shifts the power to students. Throughout this chapter, I'll describe several additional ways to encourage personal leadership in the classroom. We'll start by looking at a few fun and engaging ways to empower students to take control of their education. Then, we'll close out the chapter by considering the foundational beliefs that will help your student-led classroom thrive.

Empowerment happens when you share information and power so everyone can take initiative and make decisions. It means giving students the skills, resources, authority, opportunity, and motivation they need. It also means holding students responsible and accountable for outcomes of their actions—which will contribute to the overall success and happiness of everyone in the room. The goal is to help students use their natural curiosity and creativity to develop a passion for learning that will go with them when they leave your classroom.

GETTING PASSIONATE ABOUT LEARNING

Passion Time is one of my favorite times of the week. I feel like a proud papa watching my students fully immersed in activities of their choosing, doing things they consider valuable—all without much input from me! Seeing my students gain confidence, share their private interests so freely with their peers, and reflect so honestly is an experience I wish for every teacher who wants to know their students better. Passion Time gives me a glimpse inside the hearts and minds of each of my students. I get to know them

PASSION TIME

for who they are, not just how they perform academically. If you haven't already incorporated Passion Time into your week, I sincerely hope you will soon.

Too many children today go to school only to bide their time until they can get home and do something that truly interests them. Passion Time gives children the opportunity to spend some of the school day focusing on their personal interests and sharing those passions with others. Giving students this time is valuable in so many ways! Most children appreciate Passion Time so much that they put forth more effort into the rest of the school day. The realization that you, their teacher, care about them and their interests heightens their motivation to produce excellent work. And all the while, students are practicing the skills they need to be successful outside of school—researching, writing, planning, collaborating, revising, etc.—and enjoying the process!

MOST CHILDREN APPRECIATE PASSION TIME SO MUCH THAT THEY PUT FORTH MORE EFFORT INTO THE REST OF THE SCHOOL DAY.

Passion Time is a dedicated amount of time set aside each week for students to pursue interests. In my classroom, students are free to choose their focus without any outside influences, such as the requirement to connect it to a subject area or a specific skill. Passion Projects simply need to be approved by the teacher and follow our process, which includes a reflective blog post at the end.

"I have two children who were lucky enough to have Paul Solarz as a teacher in fifth grade. My son is now a senior in high school, and my daughter is a sophomore in high school. Paul had a unique way of creating accountability by having students lead sessions of the class studies. When my son first came home from school and told me that it was his turn to teach class' the following week, I was certain he misunderstood his homework assignment. As we talked about it further, I realized that's exactly what he was being asked to do. What I found interesting was that there was no apprehension on my son's part to conduct research to learn more about the topic and questions to facilitate learning amongst the classroom.

"It was a very memorable experience for him as he learned more about the particular subject he was 'teaching' that day and also learned the responsibility of teaching others. Both children experienced significant milestones during their fifth grade years, which made the transition into junior high very easy. Paul's method of instruction, combined with creating a classroom environment that drove higher degrees of responsibility and accountability, enabled both of my children to be more prepared for their junior high years. He also created a love for learning and opened their eyes to an infinite set of possibilities on the methods of learning that take place in and outside the classroom. Paul definitely had an impact on both of my children and their love of learning I see today."

—*Sue Nolan, Parent*

The projects my students have worked on in the past include areas of personal interest, such as sports, technology, the pseudosciences, and world history. Sometimes the subjects chosen are spurred by prior learning of, for example, natural disasters and the solar system. Others come from a desire to help animals or people, e.g., raising awareness of pit bull abuse or preventing bullying. No matter the project, the skills students learn and use during this time are extremely valuable and applicable to current classroom learning as well as their future schooling.

When I plan out my year, I schedule Passion Time twice a week for forty-five to sixty minutes each time. This time is for my students to build, create, design, research, learn, survey, etc., about topics of their choosing. Although it may sound relatively unstructured, it isn't. I simply allow my students the flexibility they need to make this time work for them. Each Passion Project can be done individually or with a partner who shares a similar interest. Although I encourage collaborative projects, I allow each student to work with a given individual only once each year. This rule encourages them to mix it up and work with others in our class.

STEP ONE: FINDING THE ESSENTIAL QUESTION

ESSENTIAL
QUESTIONS

Passion Projects begin with an "essential question" that must be approved by me. To get the go-ahead for their project, they must take a topic of interest and form it into a meaty question that can keep them actively working for a period of six weeks. Thanks to a tweet by @JohnFritzky, we now call these questions PHAT (Pretty Hard and Tough) questions. When students write PHAT questions, their next six weeks are sure to be filled with curiosity and learning.

When a question lacks depth, is too easy to investigate, or results in a dead-end, a Passion Project can quickly derail, which causes students to dislike Passion Time. Fine-tuning questions on the front end ensures students are on the right track and prevents frustration.

For example, if a student wants to learn more about the solar system, I work with her to sharpen the focus, without narrowing it so much that it becomes a question that could be answered with a simple online search. Maybe this student tells me she wants to know how the solar system began. I would tell her it's a wonderful topic but one that a quick Google search could answer. My encouragement would be for her to find several theories on how the solar system began, summarize them on video, and explain which one she thinks is the most plausible (being sure to support her answer with evidence). Now, this new direction might dampen her excitement and ruin her fun. If it does, my response would be, "If this isn't the direction you want to go, let's try something different!" If she is still interested in taking on the challenge, we pose her topic as a question such as: "Which theory do I believe is the best explanation for the beginning of our solar system?" She would then write the question on an index card, and I would draw a star on it, signaling that it has been approved.

Once an essential question has been approved, students submit them to me on a Google Form. All essential questions then populate a Google Spreadsheet that everyone in our class can view. This spreadsheet is important to me because I like to see how students improve their questions over the course of the year. Although I always have input on projects, I have noticed I spend far less time later in the year talking with students about questions that aren't PHAT enough.

While their questions improve with practice, some students run out of obvious passions as the year progresses. To maintain an idea funnel that is well-stocked with personal interests, curiosities, and passions, each student keeps a Passion Time Journal. I encourage students to write down ideas as they come up and save them for upcoming rounds of Passion Time. The journal is also especially helpful when a student gets excited about their next Passion Project before they've completed the current one. Without a place to collect their ideas, students tend to worry about forgetting a potential topic. This fear tempts them to hustle through an existing project. But with the idea safely stored for future reference, they don't seem to mind putting in maximum effort on their current project.

STEP TWO: PLANNING

Once the essential question is approved, it's time to move into the planning stage. During this time, students attempt to list the steps necessary for answering the Essential Question. Though this step can be done on paper, I prefer online planning so that, 1) we have a record of all work, and 2) project notes are easy to share. Online planning can be done in countless different ways. We use our classroom's Trello Board[1]. I like Trello because it is visually appealing, all of our "cards" are visible on the same screen, and multiple students can edit their cards at the same time.

I sign into our Trello account on one computer in the classroom, and students takes turns creating a list with all of the steps they think they will follow to complete their projects. They are required to refer to this list every time they work on their Passion Projects. Their lists, which can be updated as plans change, keep them on track and focused on what matters. Just as important, working with a plan improves their executive functioning skills. Students learn how to better manage their time, knowing that, if they "fail" and miss deadlines, they have to use their own time to catch up. Because Passion Time isn't graded, students don't associate negative feelings (remorse, shame, etc.) with missing a deadline, only a sense of responsibility, which, if you ask me, is all children *should* feel when they make mistakes!

Here is how a student's Trello card might look (each number is a step in the process):

1. Research the different theories of the formation of our solar system.
2. Explain them in my own words on video.
3. Choose the theory I think is most correct and identify specific reasons why I agree with it.
4. Explain my preferred theory on video and put all the videos together on iMovie.
5. Upload the video to YouTube.

Brainstorming and entering each step may take a student a class period or so to complete. Once the list is made, students can begin to work on those steps. I assign a hard deadline of six weeks for each project but encourage students to complete their projects early and begin working on their next project. Allowing students to stagger their finishing dates makes it easier to approve Essential Questions for the next round. Otherwise, twenty-seven students line up to talk to me at the same time! That being said, I'm also careful not to let students end too soon because that may reinforce negative behaviors (such as laziness and using shortcuts), instead of instilling grit and perseverance.

STEP THREE: DISCOVER AND BLOG ABOUT IT

As soon as their plan has been drawn up, students create a new blog entry on our classroom Passion Time blog. Although they won't finish this blog entry for several weeks, they publish their post as soon as they start working on the project, so I can watch their progress. My individualized feedback is based on what I see online; I can help them catch up, if they're behind, or encourage them to revise or improve their project, if it's done early.

This new blog entry includes the student's name and Essential Question. In addition, students begin to complete our inquiry-based version of a KWL Chart, which was originally seen on Silvia Tolisano's blog[2]. She calls it a KWHLAQ Chart. This chart incorporates finding information, taking action with the information discovered, and identifying new questions once the project is complete. (I encourage my students to continue their Passion Projects on their own, even after the six-weeks have passed. My hope is that few projects are ever "complete.")

Initially, students only fill out the first half of the KWHLAQ Chart:

- What do I already *Know*?
- *What* do I want to Learn?
- *How* will I go about learning it?

By completing these sections, students report on their background knowledge on the subject (K), identify what the focus of this project is (W), and determine the best resources to use to accomplish the focus (H). The other three columns of the KWHLAQ Chart will be completed near the end of the six weeks.

Students spend the next seven to ten Passion Time periods working on answering their Essential Question. The process of digging into their projects and discovering answers for themselves is what students love most about Passion Time. I love it too! It's exciting to watch them get in the zone and enter a world that satisfies their unique needs. They view videos, read articles, create surveys, design buildings, recreate works of art, and help those less fortunate, among dozens of other things! They crave this time because it's when they feel as if their interests are important. Bonus: Having the freedom to do something they love *every week* makes them even more appreciative of their teachers.

STEP FOUR: WRAP IT UP AND SHARE

At some point, the fun of exploration comes to a brief end. Students are required to share their learning (virtually) and reflect on the process formally, and they need to get all of this done before the deadline. In my class, the final product must include a video, a written reflection, and a completed KWHLAQ Chart.

Videos run the gamut from simple to complex. Sometimes students simply record themselves explaining the discovery process and share their findings. Other students like to take their videos up a level and create screencasts of a website they've made or record a play they've written and acted out.

The written reflection must focus on the process. Many students write about how they would do things differently next time or what challenges they came across during the project. Some students share what they learned and how much they enjoyed working on this project. Although Passion Time is not graded, I do occasionally ask my students to complete a self-assessment. The purpose is to improve the next round of Passion Time for the student, rather than assign a grade. The self-assessment helps students identify areas of strength and weakness and set improvement goals for the next round.

THE REFLECTION PROCESS REMINDS STUDENTS THAT, THE MORE WE KNOW ABOUT SOMETHING, THE MORE WE REALIZE WE DON'T KNOW!

To finish the KWHLAQ, students need to answer the remaining three questions:

- What did I *Learn*?

- What *Action* can I take? (How do I involve others in my learning?)

- What new *Questions* do I have?

These questions supplement the formal, written reflection and encourage students to do something with their newfound knowledge. Rather than quickly move on to the next project, students are encouraged to teach others (outside our classroom) about what they've learned and/or to take it a step further and actually make a difference in the world somehow. In addition, the reflection process reminds students that, the more we know about something, the more we realize we don't know! Everyone should have more questions at the end of a round of Passion Time than they did at the beginning because their background knowledge on the subject should have grown tremendously, opening their eyes to so many new thoughts and ideas!

STEP FIVE: PEER FEEDBACK

Sharing our learning with each other is a very important final step in the Passion Time process. However, I have learned that listening to twenty-seven students share topics about which they are wildly passionate can take a tremendous amount of time—and bore people who are not nearly as passionate about the subject. Therefore, I have modified the sharing process! Once all (or nearly all) of the projects for a round are complete (often a week or two past the hard deadline), we devote a class period to listening to each other's videos (independently, while wearing headphones), reading reflections, and providing helpful feedback. Here's how the review process works for my class:

To ensure every student receives feedback from at least one other person, I pull out my famous Popsicle® sticks and randomly pair students. They are required to start with their partner's video and blog entry. After leaving thoughtful comments on the blog, they can choose any other project to review. Requiring that students leave comments on every video/blog they view discourages them from just watching videos and not taking the time to provide feedback. And as you can probably guess, feedback is very important!

For every project they review, students type their feedback into the "Comments" section of the blog entry. Each year, we start by giving specific compliments, which enable students to identify aspects of their projects that were well-received by others. Everyone loves to receive compliments, so this feedback reinforces their work ethic and promotes future attention to detail. Later in the year, we add Quality Boosters to identify areas for improvement. (See "Quality Boosters" on page 96.) I make a point to stress the importance of caring about their classmates enough to process the videos well and provide feedback that will equip them to improve in the future—without hurting any feelings. This focus on helping by offering quality feedback prevents students from slacking off on one person's project in order to move on to projects they find more interesting. Fortunately, most students are very willing to give feedback on multiple projects, since they were allowed to choose videos based on their own interests. (Be sure to remind them of how lucky they are!)

For additional feedback, I ask my Twitter PLN to comment on my students' completed projects and/or to ask *their* students to leave comments. My students have loved reading comments from people around the world. Talk about an authentic audience!

PASSION TIME MINI-LESSONS

My students get so much out of Passion Time! Teaching skills in isolation doesn't work. Teaching children to do things when they're not ready doesn't work. I need an environment where I can teach a skill and have my students immediately practice it or

STUDENTS TEACHING

know they can ask other students to re-teach the skill when they are ready to use it. In my experience, it's impossible to create an environment better suited for learning than the one Passion Time provides.

In our classroom, Passion Time lasts for 60 minutes. That time includes a five- to fifteen-minute mini-lesson taught by either a student or me. My students are constantly pushing the boundaries of what children typically do in fifth grade, so these mini-lessons have become extremely important!

Let's say one student wants to learn how to record a screencast for his Passion Project final video. Other students may want to do one in the future as well, but not everyone is ready to do one today. I stop the class using "Give Me Five," ask them to close their laptops halfway to listen to my mini-lesson, and I go through the steps for making a screencast, while projecting everything on the whiteboard. Even if only one student benefits from the lesson today, the other students now have a seed planted for something they may want to do in the future. The problem is that they may not remember the steps when they are ready to screencast. In a student-led classroom, they don't need to ask the teacher to re-teach that mini-lesson. Instead, they are encouraged to do a "Give Me Five" and ask the class who could show them how to make a screencast! A handful of kids always drop what they're doing and offer to help. Interaction improves morale in the classroom, builds students' self-esteem, and improves collaboration over time. In classrooms that focus on work completion and deadlines, this kind of collaboration doesn't happen; it would cut into work time. In our classroom, students know everything is a process and revision will occur, even after the hard deadline. Brief breaks to assist a classmate in need, then, are not a nuisance but enjoyable.

At the beginning of the year, when I know a student is capable of leading the class through a mini-lesson, I ask him or her to teach the lesson. Eventually, students regularly volunteer to lead mini-lessons that they come up with independent of me! To make sure their lesson is a valuable use of time and not an attempt to focus attention on themselves, I allow them to announce they are leading a mini-lesson during Passion Time in a corner of the classroom. Students who want to learn the skill participate, and those who don't, don't. If two weeks pass and students wish they attended the mini-lesson, they can do a "Give Me Five" and ask if anyone would mind re-teaching the mini-lesson to them.

As students grow more comfortable teaching small groups, they, in time, become confident enough to lead whole-class mini-lessons. Often, I'll ask students who are doing something new and interesting if they'd be willing to teach the whole class how to do it. If they're willing, I do the "Give Me Five," announce what's about to happen, and instruct everyone to give 100 percent attention. This takes some pressure off of the student who is taking the risk to lead. They proceed to teach the mini-lesson, and I assist if needed. Over time, students request to lead mini-lessons and need less support. By the end of the year, students provide a significant portion of the instruction—and do an amazing job of it! In addition, students continue to provide small group and individual mini-lessons as needed.

By the end of the year, my students know more about each technology tool we use than I do! I teach them everything I know, but they continue teaching each other applications and workarounds that I haven't discovered—or have forgotten due to lack of use. That being said, not every mini-lesson pertains to technology. Some are procedural, some focus on specific activities students participate in (e.g. surveys, interviews, poster-creation, etc.), and some are tips and tricks for making each experience easier.

My students are encouraged to take risks, to tinker and play and experiment without fear during their learning. Freed from the fear of failure, students take more chances. They know they will receive feedback, and they've learned to graciously accept constructive criticism. No longer do they worry about imperfections or pleasing everyone all of the time. Instead, they become adventurous explorers. They don't wait for their teachers to show them the way, they blaze their own trails!

CREATING TED-STYLE VIDEOS TO SHARE PASSIONS

TED Talks have taken idea-sharing to a whole new level, allowing anyone anywhere to watch and learn (for free at TED.com) as experts and leaders present their knowledge in short, powerful speeches.

When my students choose a Passion Project topic they feel represents a strong belief, talent, or understanding, I have them prepare and deliver a speech that mimics the qualities of a TED Talk. We record the presentation from two or three camera angles in front of our green screen in our school's Production Studio, and make the background black in iMovie. We then upload the final video to YouTube and embed it on our Passion Project blog.

TED-STYLE VIDEOS

My belief is that having an authentic audience encourages students to channel their deepest thoughts and formulate passionate opinions about topics of interest to them. Writing speeches (even though they are not read verbatim) is an excellent connection to our English/Language Arts curriculum,

GREEN SCREEN FUN

and presenting the talk allows them to gain confidence and speaking skills. Students get the best of both worlds while creating TED-style videos: the ability to prepare and deliver speeches, uninhibited by a "live" audience, *and* a platform for public presentations.

EMPOWER CREATIVITY WITH MAKER SPACES

This year, I opened up my classroom to the craziness and messiness of an Imagination Club, modeled after the Maker Space[4] concept. The purpose of this after-school club is to empower kids to be kids and to make, create, design, and build! Using supplies I have scrounged up from garage sales, local businesses, and donations, students spend this time being creative and adventurous.

Other than making a plan for their creations, cleaning up after themselves, and sharing ideas and talents freely, I don't have any strict requirements or responsibilities for the club. It's simply a time for creativity and innovation—two skills currently lacking from modern curriculum. You've probably noticed that most toddlers and young children are innately curious. They ask lots of questions and like to tinker and try new things. Unfortunately, as children progress through typical schooling, their curiosity gets replaced by a fear of failure. In many school settings, students learn that setbacks are bad and should be avoided—when they *should* be learning that challenges and missteps are natural steps in any learning process.

I want students to set goals, work towards those goals, and experience setbacks along the way because that's what real life is like! Children's curiosity and creativity need to be nurtured, which is why I partnered with the Imagination Foundation[5] to create an Imagination Chapter in my school.

I WANT STUDENTS TO SET GOALS, WORK TOWARDS THOSE GOALS, AND EXPERIENCE SETBACKS ALONG THE WAY BECAUSE THAT'S WHAT REAL LIFE IS LIKE!

Our club follows a consistent schedule. Materials are put in the same spot each day and tables and desks start off in similar positions, so my homeroom students know how to set up the room for Imagination Club. Twice each week, students from other third through fifth grade classrooms join my students in the room, get their Imagination Journals, and take a seat. I teach a ten-minute mini-lesson introducing the whole-class project for the week. Students can then decide if they wish to work on that project or one of their own designs. Some students may simply want to play at one of the various stations. Whether working on a specific project or playing with arts and crafts, Legos, or Lincoln Logs, the goal is for everyone who attends Imagination Cub to find an activity that makes them happy!

The consistent format (ritual) empowers club members to take on more responsibilities throughout the year. Half of the students in our club are not from my classroom, but they quickly learn the importance of leadership and collaboration. Without asking for help or waiting for instructions, they get supplies out of the closet for others, give suggestions for project ideas, welcome new children into their groups, and even offer to record one another's reflection videos. This initiative hasn't developed by accident! Student leadership is modeled by my own students. In addition to their peers' examples, I consistently say things like, "Ask one of the students if they would mind helping you with that." Or, "I would really appreciate it if everyone in class would be willing to help each other out whenever possible so that the adults can help the students who need our help the most."

If you were a fly on the wall during our Imagination Club, you would see students choosing to stay after school to design and create things according to their own interests and curiosities. Where else can you make an elf costume out of red felt or create a foosball table out of cardboard and dowel rods? Eight- to eleven-year-olds don't generally choose to stay after school unless they are guaranteed a fun time, and these students always seem to leave fulfilled! While some students are perfectly happy playing with Legos, others push forward, challenging themselves to be more and more creative. Over the course of the school year, every student will be encouraged to take risks and seek new adventures!

Our Maker Space is not huge, expensive, or limitless. It does not have much of an electronic or technological aspect. And that's okay! There are dozens of great articles and blog posts about designing spectacular Maker Spaces. And sure, those spaces are amazing. But the reality is, most teachers don't have the budget to create huge, high-tech spaces. If that's you, start small. I encourage you to try out the Maker Space/Imagination Club concept using whatever space and resources you can find. I've learned firsthand that even small spaces and simple materials can provide a great opportunity to empower your students to grow as leaders, collaborators, makers, and dreamers!

CREATE A SAFE LEARNING ENVIRONMENT

Students come into your class under a lot of pressure! They want to impress you. They want to earn high grades. They want to maintain friendships. It's our responsibility as their teachers to minimize those pressures because students will never feel empowered in a classroom in which they feel unsafe.

Students generally want to be liked by their teachers. With this in mind, I tell my students early in the year: "If I am ever mad, disappointed, or frustrated with you and show my displeasure through my words or actions, I want you to know I still care very much about you and will not be mad for very long. Just like most teachers and parents, I have good and bad days! On a bad day, I might not respond in the most appropriate way to your actions. Just because I know what to say and do doesn't mean that I will execute it perfectly each and every time!" Children tend to blame themselves when adults are crabby. When you tell them you are having a bad day, it alleviates concern and students don't take your behavior personally. As a matter of fact, once my students know how much I care about them, they are usually extra kind to me on those tough days.

"Mr. Solarz has the class engaged not only as 'students' but as 'teachers' as they work together (with his guidance) to figure out and process information in their subjects. He uses technology in a productive way, not as a gimmick or game, but in a way that brings forth creativity and taps into each student's individual learning style. Our son did not want fifth grade to end! We were thrilled that our son, who usually did not enjoy school, loved going to school every day! Our son also matured in self-starting/completing homework and organizing his school materials. He ended the year feeling confident and prepared to enter middle school."

—*Kobra Hall, Parent*

To prepare my students for those off days when I'm crabby, we role-play potential ways to respond to me without getting upset. During the first couple of days of class, we have a short conversation: "Take a moment to imagine I am upset with you for something you did. It doesn't have to have been anything terrible, but I am upset. Visualize how I might look while I'm upset. There's a chance you may feel worried, sad, or annoyed. There's a chance that you may feel confused or concerned. Those are all understandable emotions in that situation. But I want you to know I don't want you to feel badly. Most likely, I've just made a mistake due to frustration or being overwhelmed. I can imagine that your parents have occasionally overreacted and gotten upset at you for something small. I'm sure that they wish they didn't respond that way! That's how *I* feel when that happens, as well. Let's all practice right now handling my displeasure with you without getting upset..."

I often act out the scene with a volunteer and then talk about what it felt like together as a group. It's hard to simulate a strong emotion, but I feel that taking some time to prepare them for emotional situations that might happen can only help when I make mistakes in the future. I know I'm not perfect, and I would be sad to think I've hurt my students' feelings just because I was having a bad day. We make sure to revisit this topic at least two more times throughout the year, so it's fresh in their minds. These conversations teach them empathy not only for me but for one another. Because we place significant focus on the family atmosphere of our class, students learn how to be gentle and forgiving toward each other.

EMPOWERMENT = ENJOYMENT = MOTIVATION = EFFORT = ACHIEVEMENT

When teachers empower students, the result is a higher enjoyment of learning, which leads to more motivation to work hard, which often leads to stronger achievement in class. In addition, students transfer their learning more successfully to new situations and develop the skills necessary to succeed in our constantly evolving society. But empowerment isn't just something you do. Yes, introducing projects that allow students to expand their thinking and explore their passions is important. Providing students with opportunities to make decisions and lead is critical. Real empowerment, however, comes not from activities, but from belief. As a teacher, your foundational beliefs will guide your classroom and do more to shape your students' lives than any activity ever could. I encourage you to consider each of the following beliefs. Are they part of your current teaching philosophy?

If so, terrific! Your students likely already feel as if they are an important part of the *classroom crew.*

AS A TEACHER, YOUR FOUNDATIONAL BELIEFS WILL GUIDE YOUR CLASSROOM AND DO MORE TO SHAPE YOUR STUDENTS' LIVES THAN ANY ACTIVITY EVER COULD.

If not, why not? Perhaps you've never thought about how choice or resilience could be taught or how and why to make students the experts. If one of these core beliefs hasn't been on your radar, I hope you'll be open to a new way of thinking. Because for ill or good, what you believe comes through loud and clear to your students.

Choice: Empowered students are encouraged to make choices throughout their day. Choice can mean allowing students to sit anywhere in the classroom during most activities and use any materials or technology they need to support their purposes. Since they are children, you will find yourself giving a lot of feedback in the beginning to help them make good choices. But it's worth it! Making good choices is an important skill to develop! Students need guidance and support in making wise decisions. And remember, the more choices your students have, the more empowered they will feel!

Community: Students who feel connected and cared for learn and grow together. My hope is that students feel like brothers and sisters instead of classmates. To get there, I model what it means to care about each other's well-being and talk about what it means to have one another's backs. Empower your students to stand up for their classmates in appropriate ways. They may end up arguing like siblings, but that's okay if the foundation of their relationship is solid and built on respect.

Disagreement: Differing viewpoints make learning more interesting! Much of our class is about collaboration, so there can be a false belief that everyone has to agree all the time. That's not at all true! When students work together on an assignment, my only requirement is that both sides respectfully express their opinions and listen to one another before agreeing to disagree. Students should be empowered to verbally disagree with their peers (and their teacher), so animosity doesn't breed. Classroom debates are an excellent example of disagreement at its finest!

Excitement: A classroom is a place where students should feel free to express their excitement for learning. Is your classroom a psychologically-safe learning environment? Can students get excited about upcoming lessons without being teased or put down? Tell the class how hard you work to make learning fun for them and that you hope they will show excitement for those lessons! Give immediate feedback to students who intimidate and put down others in an attempt to control their behavior. Our classroom is a place of respect and kindness. No exceptions.

Expertise: The teacher isn't the (only) expert. If you are the only person on stage every day, it will be hard for students to see you as a member of the team. They'll come to rely on you more than they should and won't take on leadership roles. In contrast, if you empower them to share their knowledge with the class and the world, they'll discover they, too, are smart enough to make decisions and solve problems on their own! My students share their knowledge with others during Passion Time, through debates and skits, and while reflecting on our simulation activities.

Impact: Students want to make an impact on their world! One of the best ways to get your students to feel empowered is to provide them with opportunities to make a difference. Service-learning opportunities and Passion Time projects are great ways to open students' eyes to the world around them. When students are encouraged to pursue causes that are near and dear to them, they learn that their place in this world matters.

Leadership: Students can capably lead themselves and others. Throughout this book, I've shared the benefits of student leadership. Empowering students to lead themselves and others results in better transfer of learning and more applicable skills for the work world. Strong leaders often learn to make smart decisions, work well with others, and are inspired to succeed. Encourage your students to work on their leadership skills, and their future teachers and employers will thank you!

Passion: Motivation grows when students love what they do. Unfortunately, most children (and adults, for that matter) struggle to identify areas as their passions. Many people go through life without being excited about anything. Empower your students to find, explore, and develop their passions. Once they discover what motivates them, they're more likely to be goal-focused and choose a career about which they're proud and excited.

Positive Self-Worth: Incremental improvement is most effective for long-term retention and personal development. When students feel judged by their grades, attentiveness, and good behavior, they may come to believe they aren't good students (or worse, aren't good people). By shifting the focus to improvement, students put forth more effort because they, too, can be successful. I make sure to tell my students how much they mean to me all the time, both collectively and individually. I regularly tell parents in front of their child how great they are, and I actually mean it. All children need to know they are cared for and that they have talent. Empowerment comes from feeling qualified and capable.

Reflection: Looking back can be a powerful tool to see the way forward. Empower your students by taking time to make meaning of what they've learned. This can be done through ePortfolio entries that include a reflective writing component. Instead of learning something and moving on quickly, take time to synthesize new learning and make it permanent in your students' minds.

Relevance: Material must be relevant to your students' lives. So much of today's curriculum makes no sense to children. It deals with concepts that are over their heads or not applicable to their lives. I always try to choose topics students can relate to, but, when that's not possible, I embed the content within a simulation or active learning experience. For example, we colonize Mars in an attempt to study the U.S. Constitution, conduct experiments to understand conductors and insulators, and have students write fictional stories about living in a state of nature. These experiences make school more relevant. If the work is meaningful to them, students will feel empowered to do their best and will ultimately remember more.

Resilience: Mistakes and failures are opportunities to grow! Empower your students to experience adversity and grow from it.

Too often, people experience setbacks and struggle to move on from them. Whether they've embarrassed themselves or made a mistake, empower children to be resilient and to come back stronger than before! In our class, whenever we do something we're embarrassed by, we say, "Own it!" That way we can laugh at our mistakes and move on.

Self-Assessment: Personal improvement over time is more important than a grade. Give your students opportunities to set goals and monitor progress towards those goals. Ask them to rate their work against criteria in a rubric or checklist. Have them identify areas where they can improve and areas that they view to be strengths. I use the Marble Theory classroom meeting to help students feel comfortable admitting they have both strengths and weaknesses. In addition, we set goals each trimester and evaluate ourselves on twenty-first century skills.

Success: Children need to hear that they are doing well! Do your students feel successful on a regular basis or are they hearing only how they need to improve? Although my students are comfortable receiving critical feedback, they need to hear positive feedback, too! Be intentional about identifying what your students do well. Point out their successes every chance you get. If you can't get to every student with positive feedback, increase the whole-class positive feedback. Kids need to be empowered to succeed, and it starts with positive feedback from their teachers!

Voice: Being allowed to speak one's mind empowers a person to develop his or her own beliefs and opinions. Make sure your students have opportunities to share their opinions and ideas with each other and with the teacher. In our classroom, students do this by evaluating various aspects of our day, rating books they read during Literature Circles, and giving feedback to their peers. Make sure you give students opportunities to share their thoughts on various aspects of the classroom as well!

Wonder: A love for learning begins with curiosity. After years of worksheets and textbooks, students gradually start to lose their wonder and excitement for learning. Two-year olds are always asking, "Why?" but school-aged children rarely do. Empower your students to regain their curiosity. Provide them with opportunities to wonder and regain their excitement for learning! I let students explore science equipment before lessons, create interesting activity names to post on the schedule, and host an after school Imagination Club to try to get my students wondering!

Learning like a pirate is an involved, all-encompassing process. Every point, from peer collaboration and improving, to teaching responsibility, to providing active learning experiences, to developing twenty-first century skills, depends on student empowerment. Without this crucial element, kids won't feel free to speak up in class or pursue what really matters to them. But you can change that! Empower them to try and fail and try again. Teach them that what's most important is becoming their personal best and helping others to do the same. Show them that it's better to fail than to never take a risk. Let your students know through your words and actions that you believe in them and in their ability to lead, improve, collaborate, grow and succeed.

Student Views on Empowerment

"This has been different from other years because we have passion time, we do 'give me fives'. Plus we have a big library! I like 'give me fives' because we get to say what we want to say without being called on. I like passion time because we get to choose what we work on, and we get to research things we like. I love the big library because I LOVE to read!!!" —*Isabela*

"I did a give me 5 that Mr. Solarz didn't like. But afterwords he said it was a risk." —*Alison*

"For our blog post for breathing through straws I didn't feel that comfortable with doing a slideshow so I decided to do an image but later on when we were taking pictures I was feeling good so I decided to take a risk because a slideshow is really nice. So I decided to go with it and it turned out really great with nice clean picture and it was very solid on the zoom to see the straw." —*Kaela*

"During Math Kendall was teacher trying to get everyone to be quiet I told people to quiet down, but other people wasn't. So I told everyone out loud in front of the class and told them to be quiet and listen to Kendall." —*Aidan*

"If you do something wrong Mr. Solarz doesn't get angry. He might after a few times of the same mistake but he'll forgive. He wants you to learn from mistakes and he does it in a good way." —*Chris*

Empowerment

1. Will you give your students the power to interrupt the class at all times, or will there be some limitations on their power?

2. What are your expectations for the rest of the class when one student is attempting to give a direction? What feedback will you provide to those who don't show respect for the leader?

3. What feedback will you provide to students who attempt to lead the class, but make mistakes, abuse their power, or monopolize the leadership opportunities?

4. What are your plans for the first day of school to ensure your classroom becomes collaborative and student-led?

5. If you aren't already, how do you plan to implement Passion Time, Genius Hour, or another form of student-choice learning into your schedule?

6. If your school doesn't already have a Maker Space for students to build, design, and create, how might you incorporate those tactile activities into your classroom?

7. What are your foundational beliefs regarding the various ways you can empower your students?

RESOURCES

1. http://www.trello.com

2. http://langwitches.org/blog

3. http://ed.ted.com/club

4. Makerspaces, STEAM labs, and fab labs are popping up in schools across the country. Makerspaces provide hands-on, creative ways to encourage students to design, experiment, build, and invent as they deeply engage in science, engineering, and tinkering. (via: Edutopia)

5. Imagination Chapters are community-organized learning spaces that foster creativity, entrepreneurship and critical twenty-first century skills in children through Creative Play. Chapters can happen anywhere—schools, homes, libraries and other community spaces—and anyone can do it. Chapters are led by volunteers from all walks of life who give a little time each week or month to help kids build the things they imagine. (via: Imagination Foundation)

OUR PURPOSE
AS EDUCATORS

"A genuine teacher does not seek to impress you with their greatness, but instead to impress upon you that you possess the skills to discover your own."

—Charles F. Glassman

I believe all teachers should allow their students to learn like pirates. Peer collaboration, placing a priority on improvement rather than grades, sharing responsibilities, providing active learning opportunities, and practicing twenty-first century skills, empowers students to become successful leaders.

Take a look at the contrasts between traditional education and PIRATE learning:

When lecture is our primary form of instruction, we reduce the time our students have to interact with each other and learn interpersonal skills. **But, when we are selective about what must be directly explained, we can create *more* opportunities for collaborative learning experiences.**

When we ask students to work independently rather than collaboratively, we turn education into an ineffective series of pass/fail assessments. **Most children need more repetition than traditional teaching methods allow. You can help students be successful by providing them with multiple opportunities to practice with and learn from their peers.**

When we reward achievement rather than improvement, students who doubt their abilities often give up because they think they'll never meet your expectations. **When we value *improvement* over achievement, students gain confidence in their current abilities *and* look forward to doing better tomorrow.**

When "good enough" is accepted by the teacher, students learn they can stop trying. **When teachers have high expectations and give personalized feedback that encourages improvement and strong effort, students rise to the occasion and often surprise themselves!**

When we don't provide our students with rituals teachers end up shouldering the leadership responsibility for the entire class. **Making parts of your class consistent allows students to anticipate the next steps and help lead others to follow them.**

When we give our students the power to lead the class but neglect to provide opportunities to do so, we fool ourselves into thinking it's the kids who are to blame for lacking leadership and drive. In reality, we are the ones who are afraid to give up control. **Create *rituals*, assign collaborative tasks, and get off the stage every day so your students have opportunities to lead.**

When teachers rely on worksheets, textbooks, and assigned seats all day, they are saying they believe passive learning is best for children. Students are not vessels to be filled with information. Students need to be active in the classroom, moving around, collaborating with their peers on meaningful assignments. "***Active learning* results in more effective development of high-level thinking processes, more effective learning, greater retention of knowledge, a higher degree of student satisfaction, and higher student self-esteem[1]."**

When we spend too much time focusing on students' acquisition of information, time devoted to acquiring much-needed, transferable skills is limited. Most information can be Googled, but most skills need to be practiced. **Spend as much of your precious class time practicing *twenty-first century skills* rather than memorizing information.**

When we see opportunities to teach our students kindness and values but pass it up because "there's just too much to do," we are saying we value academic content more than character. **Life lessons are what our students need most, and life lessons are what they will carry with them forever.**

When we teach our students to ask permission before making decisions, expect them to wait for directions, and shame them when they make mistakes, students learn to obey rather than lead. We are not teaching stray dogs how to behave; we are teaching the future leaders of America how to be responsible decision-makers. *Empower* **your students to take risks and make decisions without your prior approval. Only then will they gain the confidence they need to lead!**

SINCE EACH DAY IN CLASS MIMICS REAL LIFE, STUDENTS CAN SEAMLESSLY APPLY THE SKILLS THEY LEARN IN SCHOOL TO REAL-WORLD SITUATIONS.

Watching your students mature over the course of the school year is one of the real joys of being a teacher. Knowing what they were like those first few weeks and understanding what they've become by those last few is something in which you can take pride. When students participate in a student-led classroom for a full year, they leave with an unmistakable, newfound confidence. As they proceed through their school years, these students bravely take risks, make decisions in their groups, and help others when they see the need.

Even those who are naturally shy or introverted learn to overcome challenges and lead by example with a positive attitude.

Student-led classrooms offer countless benefits to students—and to teachers! At the heart of all those benefits, however, is the reality that developing personal responsibility and learning how to work with others prepares students for life! When children participate in a student-led environment, they feel more connected to their learning. They come to accept their teacher as one member of the team, rather than their boss, because everyone shares the power and the responsibilities equally. School becomes more fun! Interpersonal relationships improve as students learn and practice social skills most of each day. Everyone's opinion matters and everyone's voice is heard. Intrinsic motivation drives students because they are invested in their education. Improvement becomes the collective focus, and grades take a back seat. Students show pride in their work but are even more proud of their growth. Confidence grows. Soon students are taking educated risks, sometimes failing, but always willing to try again. Failure is not a deterrent, it's a positive motivator. Since each day in class mimics real life, students can seamlessly apply the skills they learn in school to real-world situations. Students leave a student-led classroom changed. They appreciate everything their teacher did for them, but they are no longer reliant upon them. They are independent thinkers, capable of handling anything that comes their way!

How could any teacher not want that for his or her students? Empowering students *is* our purpose and responsibility. I hope you'll use the ideas in *Learn Like a PIRATE* to re-spark your excitement for teaching and be the positive influence that your students

CONSUMERS/ PRODUCERS

need and deserve! The fulfillment you'll experience as you watch them grow will be worth the effort. I promise.

I hope you will connect with me on Twitter, on my website, via email, or at an education conference, because we learn the most when we collaborate with each other. I absolutely *love* sharing what I'm doing with others, but I'm even happier when I find a new idea I can use in my classroom. I can't spend all of my time re-inventing the wheel, and, thankfully, I don't have to because my PLN shares amazing ideas every single day online! I sincerely hope to learn from you in the near future. Please share all the great things you're doing in your classroom with others. And *please*, continue to create a student-led classroom!

Twitter: @PaulSolarz
E-Mail: psolarz@sd25.org
Website: LearnLikeAPirate.com

Resources

[1] Source: (Kulik & Kulik, 1979; Smith, 1977; Johnson et al., 1998; Slavin et al., 1985; Rau & Heyl, 1990; McKinney & Graham-Buxton, 1993). http://www.academia.edu/1969321/Active_Learning_to_improve_long-term_knowledge_retention

ALSO FROM

DAVE BURGESS
Consulting, Inc.

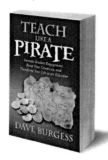

Teach Like a PIRATE
Increase Student Engagement, Boost Your Creativity, and Transform Your Life as an Educator
By Dave Burgess (@BurgessDave)

Teach Like a PIRATE is the *New York Times'* best-selling book that has sparked a worldwide educational revolution. It is part inspirational manifesto that ignites passion for the profession, and part practical road map filled with dynamic strategies to dramatically increase student engagement. Translated into multiple languages, its message resonates with educators who want to design outrageously creative lessons and transform school into a life-changing experience for students.

P is for PIRATE
Inspirational ABC's for Educators
By Dave and Shelley Burgess (@Burgess_Shelley)

Teaching is an adventure that stretches the imagination and calls for creativity every day! In *P is for Pirate*, husband and wife team Dave and Shelley Burgess encourage and inspire educators to make their classrooms fun and exciting places to learn. Tapping into years of personal experience and drawing on the insights of more than seventy educators, the authors offer a wealth of ideas for making learning and teaching more fulfilling than ever before.

Pure Genius
Building a Culture of Innovation and Taking 20% Time to the Next Level
By Don Wettrick (@DonWettrick)

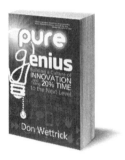

For far too long, schools have been bastions of boredom, killers of creativity, and way too comfortable with compliance and conformity. In *Pure Genius*, Don Wettrick explains how collaboration—with experts, students, and other educators—can help you create interesting, and even life-changing, opportunities for learning. Wettrick's book inspires and equips educators with a systematic blueprint for teaching innovation in any school.

Ditch That Textbook
Free Your Teaching and Revolutionize Your Classroom
By Matt Miller (@jmattmiller)

Textbooks are symbols of centuries of old education. They're often outdated as soon as they hit students' desks. Acting "by the textbook" implies compliance and a lack of creativity. It's time to ditch those textbooks—and those textbook assumptions about learning! In *Ditch That Textbook*, teacher and blogger Matt Miller encourages educators to throw out meaningless, pedestrian teaching and learning practices. He empowers them to evolve and improve on old, standard, teaching methods. *Ditch That Textbook* is a support system, toolbox, and manifesto to help educators free their teaching and revolutionize their classrooms.

ABOUT THE AUTHOR

Paul Solarz has been teaching fifth grade at Westgate Elementary School in Arlington Heights, Illinois, since 1999. He advocates for student-centered teaching practices and a focus on twenty-first century skills attainment. Fortunately for Paul, his school and district administration have given him plenty of autonomy to take risks and be innovative over the years. This has led to his unique style of teaching and the motivation to share his strategies with the broader education community.

Recently, Paul was named a Top 50 Finalist for the Varkey GEMS Global Teacher Prize. The Global Teacher Award seeks to do for education what the Nobel Prize has done for science, literature, and peace. He was also named the 2014 Educator of the Year by ICE (Illinois Computing Educators) for effectively integrating technology in his classroom. He earned his master's degree in Curriculum and Instruction from Illinois State University and is a National Board Certified Teacher. He also earned his bachelor's degree in Elementary Education from Winona State University in Minnesota.

CPSIA information can be obtained at www.ICGtesting.com
Printed in the USA
BVOW04s0301201015

423196BV00002B/4/P